NEW PLAINS REVIEW
SPRING 2021

New Plains Review
Spring 2021

University of Central Oklahoma

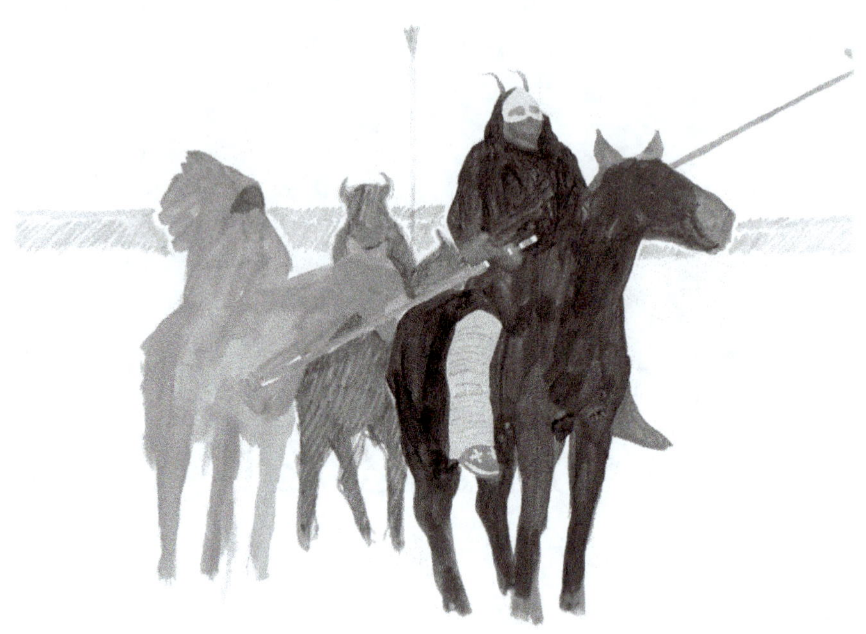

Phantom Warriors
Sherman Chaddlesone

New Plains Review is edited by students and faculty of the English Department in the College of Liberal Arts at the University of Central Oklahoma. The political, social, or artistic commentary represents the views of the writers and artists, and inclusion in the journal does not indicate editorial endorsement or non-endorsement.

New Plains Review does not claim to represent the views of the University of Central Oklahoma.

The image found on the previous page is from a painting titled Phantom Warrior by acclaimed Native American artist and UCO alumnus Sherman Chaddlesone (Kiowa).

Visit our website at newplainsreview.com

Email inquiries to newplainsreview@gmail.com

Mailing Address:
New Plains Student Publishing
University of Central Oklahoma
100 N University Drive, Box 184
Edmond, OK 73034

Publishing in the USA; pricing & manufacturing information can be found on the final page. First Printing, 2021.

Masthead

FACULTY & STAFF

Executive Editor
Shay Rahm

Production Chief
Lana Riana Jones

EDITORIAL BOARD

Co-Editors-in-Chief
Zoe Wright
Paul Rainwater

Senior Editors
Bailey Dickey
Edward Callery
Anthony Cooper
Kobi Hampton
Kyle Major
Timi Matlack
Rebekah Kitzrow

Assistant Editors
Lexi Brown
Kathryn Brown

Korbyn Carter
Abigail Griffin
Courtney Hamm
Kari Hampton
Cayla Lane
Dakota Mayes
Sierra Montgomery
Riley Taylor
Kellen Welch
Bradley Wood

Director of Digital Content
Timi Matlack

Director of Social Media
Paul Rainwater

Digital Content & Social Media Managers
Katie Brown
Edward Callery
Korbyn Carter
Bailey Dickey
Abigail Griffin
Kobi Hampton
Cayla Lane
Sierra Montgomery
Bradley Wood

Director of Communications
Zoe Wright

Communications Specialists
Edward Callery
Anthony Cooper
Kellen Welch

Contents

Good Housekeeping: Baby's Center

KATHERINE GAFFNEY

Remember the tulle and patches,
the waists blooming and the linings
teething. Now remember the warm

hen in her coop with her perfect
brown eggs beneath her. Remember
the rabbit you learned to behead,

the way your grandfather pushed
you to skin the brown hair to purple
flesh. Remember the tears you cried

for stamping out a life, remember too
his reason. That rabbits multiply.
Do not forget that you, now,

are multiplying too, that the belly
that grows is growing a great stone
weight for you to heave, will soon

deflate a satchel of wrinkles
for you to rub cream and potions
over to try to find the skin you

remember before this life making
began, the weight gain, fertility
found in the thicket of uncertainty

over whether your body would labor
as fruitlessly for so many babies
as your mother. Genealogy is the work

of translating map to wilderness,
to see what truths make it
from the theoretical extraction

or what changes nature has made
between drawing and trudging.
He will be there, as he was

when you two joined to begin filling
in the yellow and aged, blank paper,
to see how easily you could accomplish

this work of genealogy. He will be
there, not behind the bulky camcorder
your father had to keep replacing

with new cassettes as your mother
never dilated, as she and the doctor
prepared for an epidural. The distance

of experience through a lens. As you
allowed the distance of the shift
from coop to table to not consider

the imminence of life in an egg,
brewing lives in the doe's womb.
The doe, the female rabbit,

your grandfather never meant to kill,
the womb filled with kits not done
stewing. All the potential shots

your grandfather wouldn't fire. The brief
fire in the shot down your mother's spine,
her only hope of extracting the one

life she carried this far. He took over
the extraction of the kits from the now
still life womb. His garage was a still

life, of hanging pelts and knives and skulls
dried clean and milky. Unlived lives of this
womb stopped, mid cycle, not unlike

the lives ranging from bloody mess
to fleshy nut that fell from your mother
over a toilet or pulled from her on a table

as your grandfather pulls the nutty kits
from the doe. He who shares your bed
will be there as your father wasn't when

the waxy blue paper wafted over
your mother's belly, as the doctors
sunk their scalpels past her muscles

to the womb that had no escape
and pulled you, red, weighted
as the rabbit you learned to skin.

Rainbow Woman

ERIKA MARIA

COVER ARTIST - NEW PLAINS REVIEW
SPRING 2021

Artist's statement

In my current work, I intend to capture people's unique expressions, gestures, and movements. My art is representational, but I aspire to create more abstract color palettes and deconstructed forms.

Since realizing I had some drawing skills as a child, I knew my life's work would have to include art in some way. But it wasn't until I started painting as an adult, that I knew I could use it to communicate the human spirit. Art is not just something I do, it is who I am, and part of my identity. Painting has given me an energy and purpose to life. I believe there is a loneliness that comes with being human. For me art has been a way of surviving, it has always made being alone not so lonely. When I realized this about myself, I started taking an interest in exploring the ideas and feelings humans have with being alone. I aspire to connect to my audience through my art, in hopes of promoting how we are all more alike than we are different. I want my work to evoke an emotion.

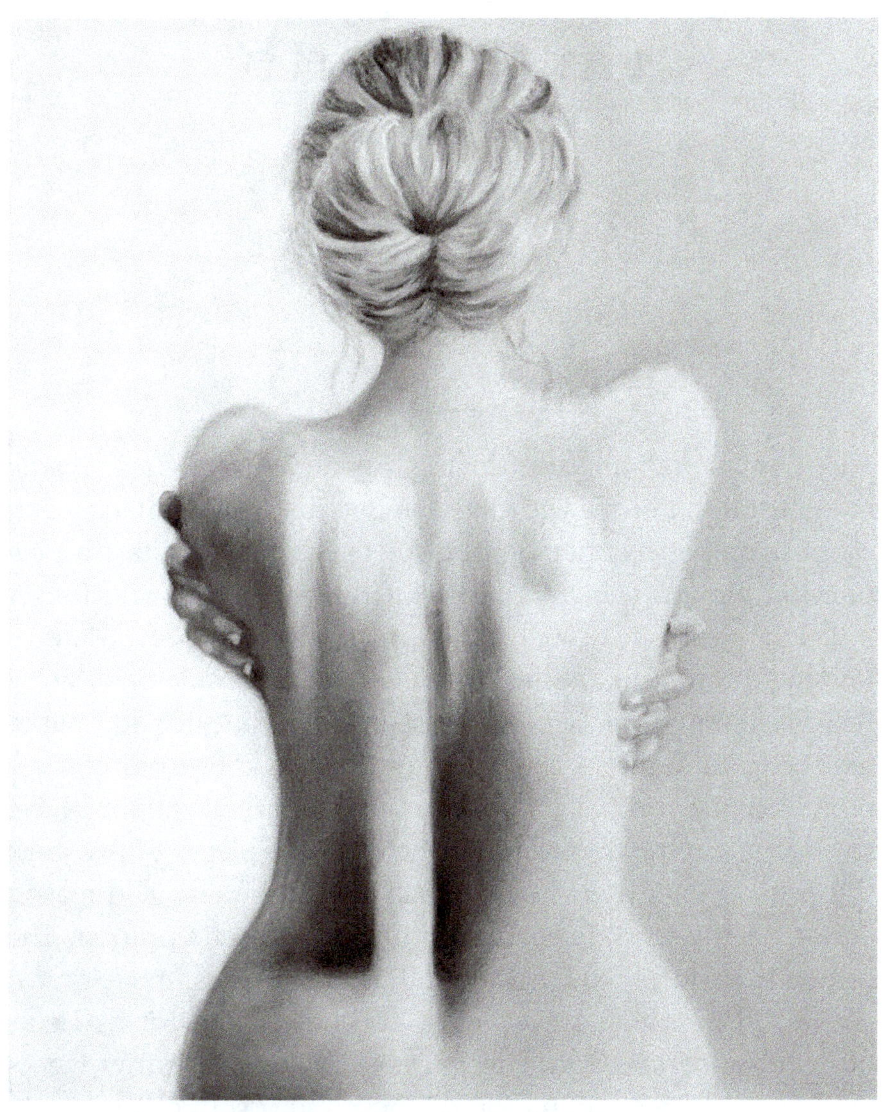

Rainbow Woman, Feb 2021 - Oil on Canvas (16x20)
Erika Maria

"Rainbow Woman
I don't think she knows how special she is.
I don't think she knows...
She could have done anything she ever wanted in this world."

On the Earth

OLGA NENAZHIVNA

Artist's Statement

I work in all mediums, but mainly ink and paper. These media are natural materials with live energy. Just like humans, each sheet of paper has personal differences. Before I start a new drawing, I put a sheet of paper in front of myself and I start a dialogue with it. I touch the surface, check the structure to understand its capabilities. Then I choose the side on which I will draw. Daily practice has reassured me that ink and paper are the most suitable media for me. Each and every thing created in this world has its own name and purpose and if I have to choose a name that would unite all of the pieces of my work into one whole, then I would name it chronicle. The reason driven by my work is that I genuinely enjoy the process, the outcome and the feedback I get. For many years I have drawn the world in which I live, and I continue. I draw it as I see, feel and understand it. The images that appear in my works are born from a combination of these factors. In other words, I do not come up with images and plots, they are a product of this world. To some, it may appear that figures and objects from my drawings are fantasy, but this is only a point in extent at which many factors intersect and form a "thoughtform". A load of images and objects, their certain sequential arrange-ment - all this creates a special spirit of the drawing. This is a philosophical and aesthetic work of art. My artwork is a friend and a partner. It will "talk" to you, and with each new sight, you will discover new facets in it.

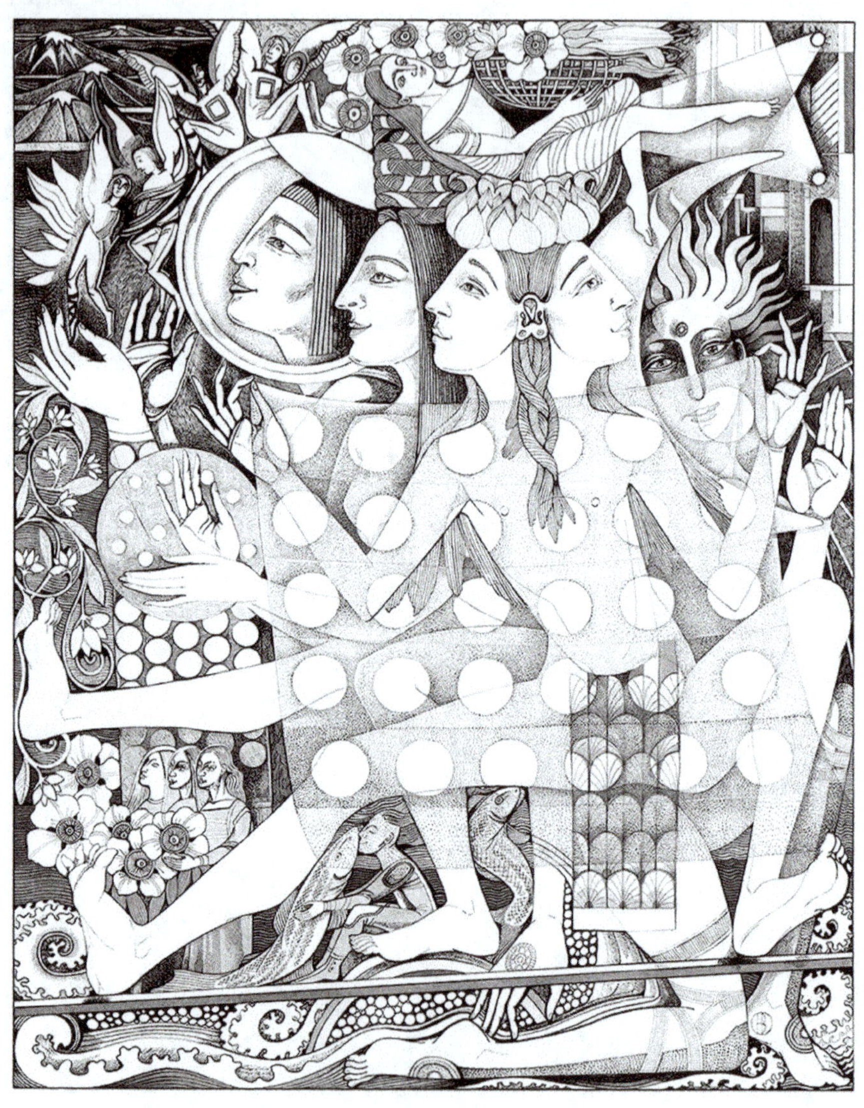

On the Earth I, 2020 - Ink on paper, 14x11 in. (35.5x28 cm.)
Olga Nenazhivna

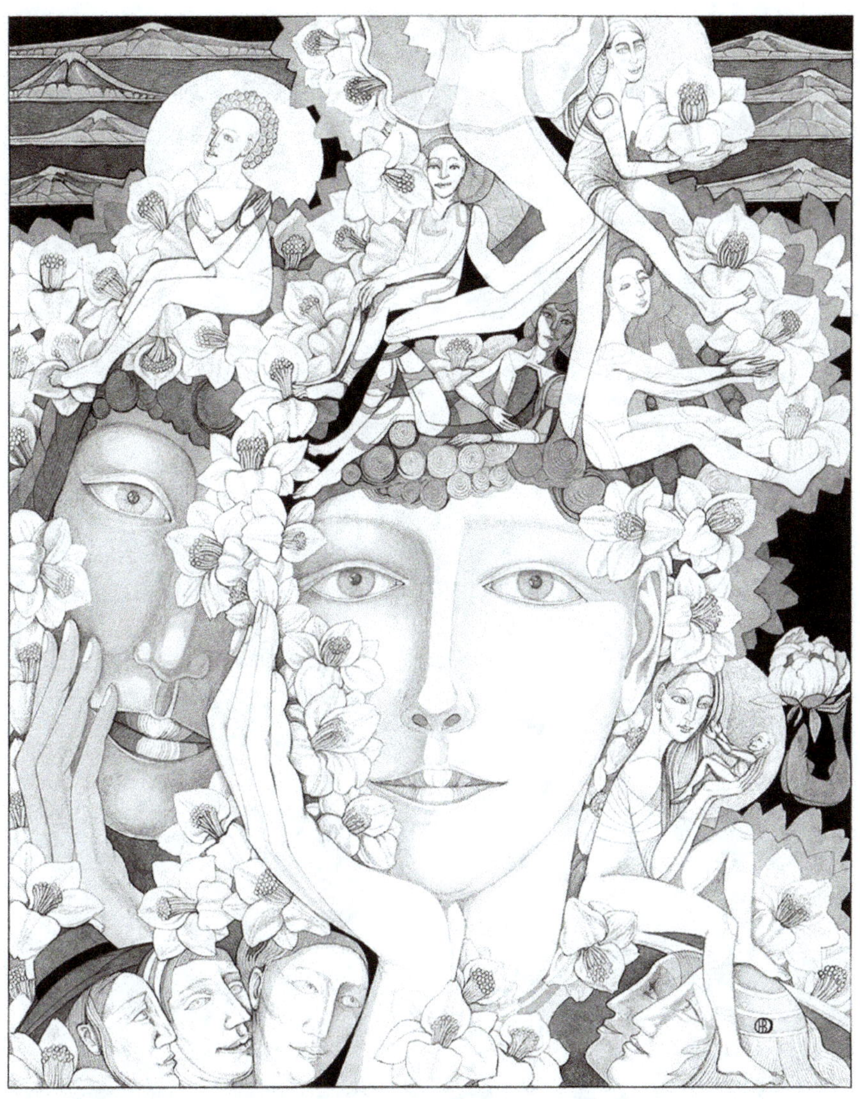

On the Earth II, 2020 - Ink on paper, 14x11 in. (35.5x28 cm.)
Olga Nenazhivina

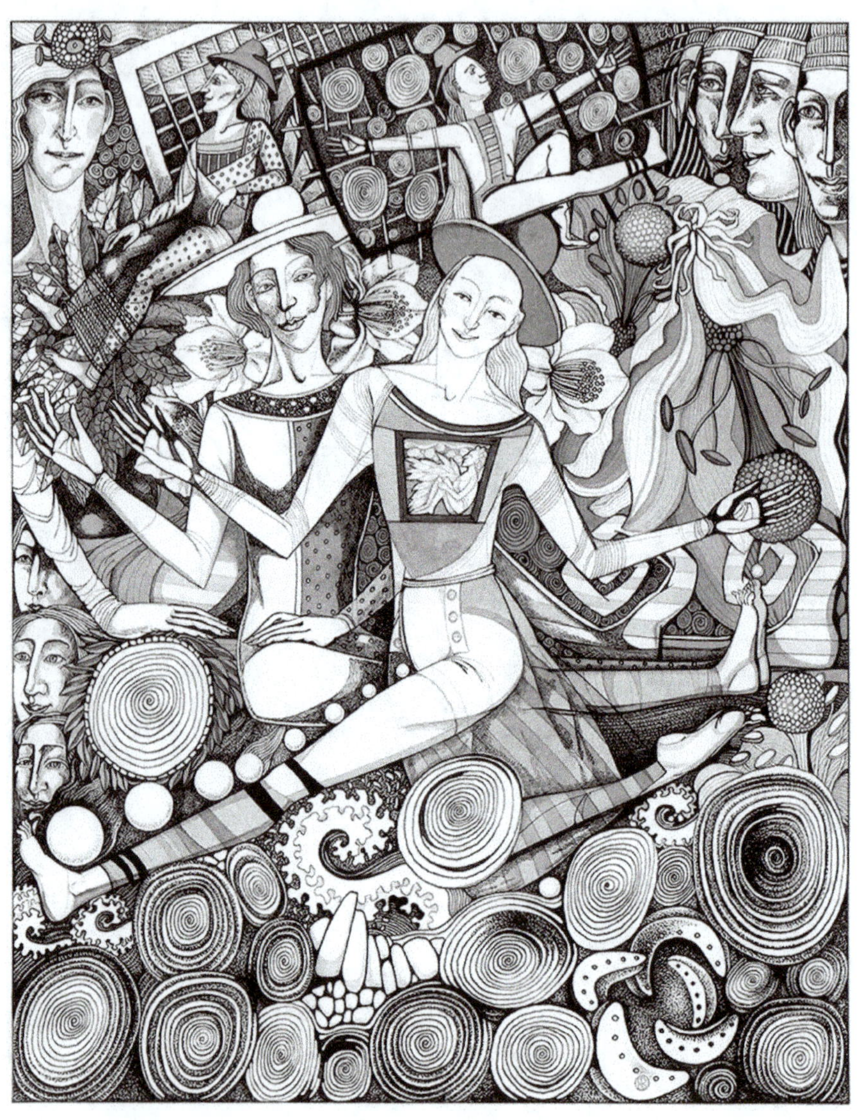

On the Earth III, 2020 - Ink on paper, 14x11 in. (35.5x28 cm.)
Olga Nenazhivina

Three Poems: Today I, Portrait of Hong Kong, The Robin Is Still Beautiful

KAITLIN KAN

Today I

Today I masturbated on the floor of a psych ward bathroom.
It was hard and cold
like my nipples beneath my paper pajama shirt,
studded with goosebumps in January hoar.
Getting caught in bed would've been an indignity too great,
greater even than being deemed too reckless for
pens
shampoo
a stuffed animal
loved ones.
Throbbing between my legs
all the desperation I could not show
lest they sniff out the openings in my facade
that too much betray my tenderness.
It's the softest parts of the soul they're after,
to medicate them, make them turgid, untouchable.
But even in madness
I still crave the touch of romance and soft intrusions alike.
    I came quickly and quietly in the bleached morning air.

Portrait of Hong Kong

I weave through the trunks of family trees
whose branches knit in matrimony
quite over canopying the ivy-clad mountain
where skyscrapers protrude like teeth.
Still a mere flâneur on the shores of heredity,
where I peeled lychees like lanterns
and bowed to the ashes of ancestors,
whiteness coating my tongue,
choking on the cantonese I wasn't taught.
A city floating in a perfume of decay
from the carcasses hanging in the meat stalls
and the offshore hands that softly suffocate
the lives willed to us in nucleotides.
Finding small joys in the liminal spaces,
where I am both loved and unknown
in the stories I can share with no one,
leaves fall in the wake of my stroll about the Peak
as I bear fruit with my words
whose juices paint the smog over a lazy sunrise,
overhanging the breath-congested strand.

The Robin Is Still Beautiful

Just as they told me
to cleanse myself of clichés,
he bathes in a pool of melted snow;
the robin is still beautiful.

Even when the snow has lost its iceblink
to the slow death of hoary-headed February,
taking flight from the snowbank's grime;
the robin is still beautiful.

Though a weary life becomes me
as I wrestle with my own decay,
cutting through the neural mist on crimson-crested wings;
the robin is still beautiful.

From behind the bars of my trappings
woven in and around my shame-ridden body
I watch him tend his feathers in avian pride;
the robin is still beautiful.

Hobson's Choice

DAVID ZARKO

Characters

JOYCE
Thirty-four, is a bit stout and pretty. She has small patience
for hedging the truth.

TROY
A dancer, lithe, about thirty, gay, yearning for simplicity.

Setting

A stoop in New York's Hell's Kitchen.

Time

Summer, 1995

Hobson's Choice

*Joyce is sitting on the top step reading a Donna Leon novel and
leaning against a planter.
She wears reading glasses. Her cordless handset rings, she puts
down her book and clicks on.*

JOYCE

Hello, Joyce speaking. Hey, Mom. Fine, fine, how are you? Sitting on the stoop reading. It's like a porch. I got a cordless. Phone? Right, one of those things with an antenna. Sure it works, I live on the first floor. It's safe. Not a cloud in the sky. I won't get electrocuted. No, I'm not afraid of being assaulted. It's still daylight. Almost five o'clock. Yeah, two hours ahead. It's always two hours. How would it randomly change? You're remembering wrong. No, that wasn't a criticism. I don't know yet, maybe go to a movie. It's Saturday. No, I don't work on Saturday. I never have. Once, about three years ago, *once* I worked on a Saturday. Yeah, you're right, it could happen again. Mom, this is New York, there are tons of movie theaters, we'll be able to get in. Anyway, what's up? Well, that's nice, it's good to hear your voice, too.

Troy comes out, gives Joyce a kiss on the head, and sits next to
her.
He's dressed in shorts and flip flops.

Yeah, I'll be home late August. I know it's hot there in August, but it's hotter here. It's dry heat there, here it's really, really, *really* muggy. No, I don't mind the snow. The city, the landlord, so long as *I* don't have to shovel it. We'll talk about weather when I get home, okay? I got three weeks off work. No, I can't stay there the whole time, just... well, maybe six days. Sure, I love seeing you and Dad, but... I need a vacation. No, a vacation is a cottage in the woods in Ontario, some place new, unfamiliar. Yes, if I change my mind you'll be the first to know. I should go. Hug Dad for me. Love you.

TROY

You don't fight with her.

                                    JOYCE

No, but I feel like I've been thrown into a dumpster full of
fly paper.

                                    TROY

I fight with mine.

                                    JOYCE

I know, and you gotta stop or you'll hate yourself when you're
sixty.

                                    TROY

(*pause*) Plans?

                                    JOYCE

Movie night?

                                    TROY

I dunno. Nothing I wanna see.

                                    JOYCE

Thirty movies playing within five blocks and there's nothing
you wanna see?

                                    TROY

It's mostly summer stuff.

                                    JOYCE

There's always the Angelika or Lincoln Plaza. I'll get the paper...

TROY

I looked. There's the E.M. Forster flick, Merchant Ivory festival at the Angelika. But ya know, it's warm, it's Saturday!

JOYCE

Air conditioned comfort on a sweltering Saturday night sounds okay by me. Say you don't wanna go to a movie.

TROY

I just did.

JOYCE

You said everything but "I don't wanna."

TROY

Okay, I don't wanna. Maybe I'll go to the health club, work-out, swim.

JOYCE

I can go to a movie alone. Not the first time.

TROY

If you'd join the health club, you could come with me. You know, you're getting a little...

JOYCE

Yeah, say it.

TROY

Zaftig?

                              JOYCE

You're not Jewish, I'm not Jewish, how can I be zaftig?

                              TROY

You maybe could.

                              JOYCE

Maybe could what?

                              TROY

Use it.

                              JOYCE

Use what?

                              TROY

Maybe a little exercise.

                              JOYCE

Right, I'm to blame.

                              TROY

For what?

                              JOYCE

Your seven-month itch. Used to be seven years but we're all experience-junkies these days.

                              TROY

That's so cliché.

                              JOYCE

What's the longest time you've gone without kissing a man?

                              TROY

Lips?

                              JOYCE

Tongues.

                              TROY

Before last Christmas? Three weeks?

                              JOYCE

And after seven months, you itch. Seems normal enough to me.

                              TROY

(*brief pause*) Do you think we've reached a limit?

                              JOYCE

Do you?

                              TROY

I think I asked you first.

                              JOYCE

How would I know? It's your limit. You're gorgeous, you're
sweet, watching you walk around the apartment is like watch-
ing a painting by Gauguin set to music.

TROY

And?

JOYCE

Okay. Yeah. (*pause*) It's not enough being friends who cuddle.

TROY

You said the plumbing issue was trivial.

JOYCE

Up to a point. I turn thirty-five next week.

TROY

Why are we talking about this on the stoop?

JOYCE

No a/c. It's barbaric. I'm a valued legal temp, you're a some-times Broadway dancer...

TROY

Little by little, we're settling down.

JOYCE

...how can we not have the money for a lousy air conditioner?

TROY

I don't like the whole scene thing. I hate dating. (*pause*) I've been happy these past few months.

                              JOYCE

I know.

                              TROY

You?

                              JOYCE

Basically.

                              TROY

So?

                              JOYCE

You haven't got the same clock, Troy. You can change your
mind about family when you're seventy if you can find a girl
who likes you. I haven't got that option.

                              TROY

And if I exit the scene, you will?

                              JOYCE

Not like there's someone else waiting, bouquet in hand, no.
(*pause*) I just don't think we're ever gonna bond so much that
you stop... you stop looking at guys.

                              TROY

I don't *look*. It's aesthetic appreciation.

JOYCE

It's the same like a regular boyfriend looking at girls. The depth of desire isn't a factor.

TROY

Regular?

JOYCE

I'm either getting serious with someone or I'm going to cultivate strange habits so I can be an eccentric old maid who's funny instead of pathetic. I'm behind schedule on both counts. I cannot live with the notion that I'm gonna wake up one morning to find a dented pillow, no note, and your tight jean drawer cleared out.

TROY

I thought we were serious.

JOYCE

(*brief pause*) How about you'll be out by the end of the month.

TROY

Can't we give this a couple days' thought?

JOYCE

We've done more than a couple days. (*pause*) It's easier talking to you than my mother.

TROY

I'm sorry if I don't...

JOYCE

Listen. Do you really expect to be satisfied with me? By me?

TROY

I'd like to try.

JOYCE

If you still have to try after seven months... I'm not a car you have to get used to because you can't afford to trade it in.

TROY

People always used to get used to each other, make do, find ways of compromising and...

JOYCE

I think we're moving past that.

TROY

There is something sweet about a couple in an arranged marriage who learn to accept...

JOYCE

I mean as a society. There. It's not sexual, it's sociological. Feel better?

TROY

No.

JOYCE

Were you ever in love with Richard?

TROY

Sometimes. Yeah. No, only when I got drunk. Or lonely. I dunno. Maybe. That was years ago.

JOYCE

Marc?

TROY

I fall in love with all my friends when I first meet them.

JOYCE

Let's define terms. Pretend they apply to me. In love.

TROY

I think about you a lot, feel a kind of rush when we meet.

JOYCE

Infatuated.

TROY

I think about you way too much and can't speak full sentences when we meet.

JOYCE

Plain love.

TROY

(*brief pause*) I don't think about you at all and feel like we're the most interesting people on earth when we're together.

                              JOYCE

Which am I?

                              TROY

Guess.

                              JOYCE

That's nice. How does that get me a kid?

                              TROY

You're sure you want a kid?

                              JOYCE

Right at this moment? I don't know. But my mind could change
about that in ten seconds. And if it does, I don't want to have
to reorganize my whole life to get pregnant.

                              TROY

We adopt. They plant a fertile egg. We find a guy to volunteer.
I take a pill. It's 1995, there are loads of options out there.

                              JOYCE

Yeah. I dunno. Maybe the plumbing is an issue after all. And
you know why I don't join your health club.

                              TROY

Yeah, well, it's only been seven months, lots of stuff to get
used to.

                              JOYCE

You've been on the road for three. This is not how I imag-
ined things would turn out. (*pause*) Marc was in love with you.
Probably still is.

                              TROY

Yeah, a crush.

                              JOYCE

Define.

                              TROY

I think about you all the time, and say stupid things when we
meet. Really, embarrassingly stupid things. Which am I?

                              JOYCE

None of the above. Best friend.

                              TROY

Define.

                              JOYCE

You cross my mind all by yourself sixteen times an hour, and
when we meet it's like being with myself, only not lonely.

                              TROY

You, too.

                              JOYCE

Did you go through being in love with me?

TROY

The shortest being in love in history. Between when Richard introduced us, and the end of dinner. By the time we got back from that play... what was it?

JOYCE

The Ideal Husband.

TROY

Good memory. By the time we went for drinks, I'd known you all my life.

JOYCE

Yeah. Okay. Me, too.

TROY

But you want babies via regular, socially acceptable, Mom-blest techniques. (*pause*) How about we go see *Maurice*? It's at the Angelika.

Joyce looks at him for a long time.

I do love you, best friend.

JOYCE

I hate you. Why can't we be normal?

TROY

Define.

                              JOYCE

Functional plumbing.

                              TROY

There's more to life than romance.

                              JOYCE

Define.

                              TROY

Falling in love, crushes, infatuations... plain love with candles.

                              JOYCE

Did I think maybe you'd flip?

                              TROY

I kinda thought I might.

                              JOYCE

So, it's your fault. Good. You deserve better. Get dressed, I
wanna finish this chapter.

                              JOYCE

Hi Mona, it's me. Yeah. Well, yes, you're right. It's that obvious?
I know, but it doesn't matter how long you think about some-
thing, when it finally happens... Going to see *Maurice* with

Troy. I know. Probably not the best thing, but when he suggested it, "no" exited my vocabulary. I'll be okay. Just a touch incredibly sad and a little totally desperate, but it'll pass in a couple of years. I'm reading... um...

She picks up her book to check the cover...

Death in a Strange Country. Yeah, that is kind of the loneliest possible concept imaginable. Or maybe the next loneliest. Uh-huh. Uh-huh. Just a sec, Mona.

While she exits, yelling...

Troy? (*to Mona*) I'll call you later. (*disconnects*) How about the end of next week?

Lights out.

Facing it Together

JACK BORDNICK

Artist's Statement

My sculptural and photographic imagery is a reflection of my past and present forces and the imagination of my life's stories. They represent an evolutionary process of these ideas and how that all of life's forces are interconnected, embraced, and expressed thru creative art forms. My works, represent what I have accomplished with this art form. I call it my quantum and metaphoric moment, the changing from one form to another. They express and implement my thoughts and feelings, regarding taking risks, without any guarantee of their success..... and to be reflected in these present works, is my goal. The predominant imagery deals mostly with faces of both living and non-living beings and things. They are expressed in these many forms and images and do speak to us in their own languages.

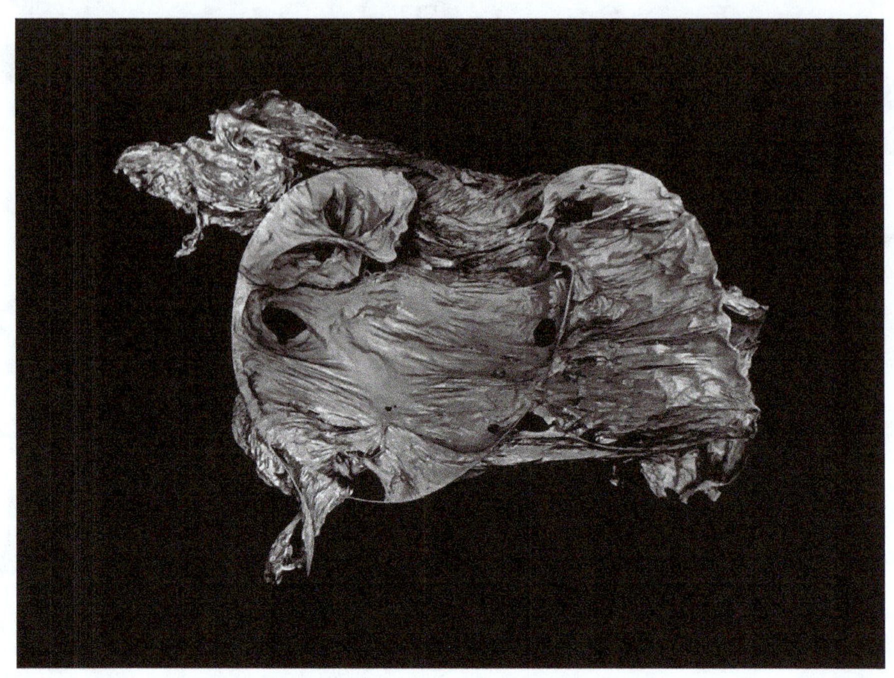

Facing It Together Series, 2020 - Mixed Media (24 x 14 x 2)
Jack Bordnick

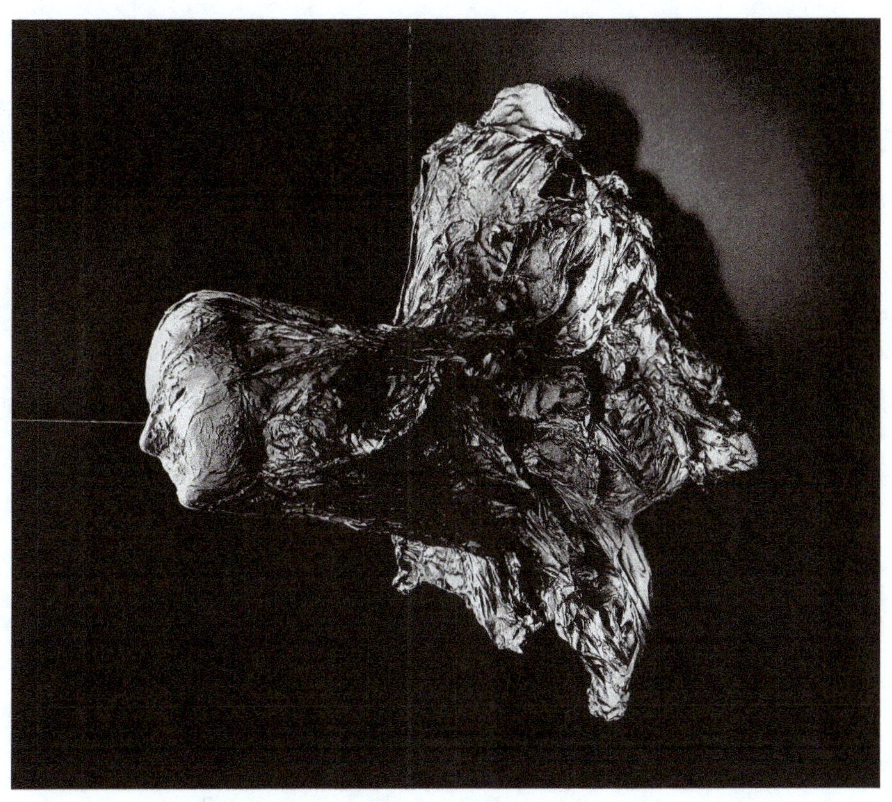

Facing It Together Series, 2021 - Mixed Media (24 x 24 x 28)
Jack Bordnick

Secondhand Life

ANGEL M. BAKER

We had lots of clothes indeed. We wore hand-me
down jeans and sweaters, lopsided and
lived in. Those clothes held memories of prior bones
like warm pitted fruit. I heard mother say, *Tooth and nail*,
as she worked sewing fabrics together, reams quartered

by yard, to make us clothes, too. *What's the most
durable, the toughest*, mother asked a clerk, as
I'd play in the stacks, hiding in canvas, tulle, pastoral
patterns of country sides. She once made me a dress
of eyelet and flowers for special occasions.

I wore it around the house pretending I was a poet. The
kind of naturalist that surveyed the order of things.
*The old clothes are for chores and playing with your
brothers*, mother said. My fingers dawdled about the
bobbin, zippers latched and unlatched at the exhausted Singer.

My brothers were older and didn't learn to sew. Their
bodies fit into clothes like half drained bags of sugar.
Their limbs swam around the loose fabric but
they had to act big so no one could tell
those were dead men's clothes. We walked through

our lives pretending to belong in our bodies,
our clothes hanging on us in the pretend way
I performed surgery on toys. (If you don't pretend,
there's no telling what might happen.) It was a great
joy to wear my big brother's t-shirts. They had logos

of cars and surfing and hung down below my knees and
gave me magical powers. I could skateboard, run
for miles to the gas station for gum, hurl myself up to
the top bunk to imagine my stuffed animals come to life.
Mother wore long smocks that I saw artists wear in movies.

Her body held the draped fabric like cracked stone,
but her hands seemed the most used up, the most
tired. Skin shifted over tendon, threaded needles, kneaded
dough, braided my long hair. When her hands
were tired, they smoked cigarettes and rubbed into

each other. You could hear them whisper, *I'm worn
down to the bone.* I told my brothers we should
protect mother's bones and not be any trouble. I looked at
my own hands – they didn't look so tired – and I thought,
I won't be any trouble.

This second hand life fits me alright.

Money Shot

ROBERT MCGUILL

He was gentle, that was his way. But it was the kind of gentle that got its way. He wasn't one to try and break you, outright. He never raised his voice, much less a hand. What he preferred instead was a prolonged and thoughtful silence, or at most a lingering stare, to win out, or over, whatever obstacle opposed him. So when he called me that night and told me he'd been arrested for putting a boy in the hospital after beating him with a baseball bat, I didn't believe it.

"Connor?"

"I'm here," I said, trying to shake the picture from my head.

"Look," he said, "I don't want to get into it over the phone. There's no point. The important thing is, he's going to recover, and anyway, that's not why I'm calling."

Father and I hadn't talked to one another in something close to a year, and our last face-to-face had been even longer. Long before the letter letting me know he and Mother had decided to divorce. I'd only recently been appointed the head of the film studies department of a small private college in Iowa—the same college he and Mother attended when they were young—and the move to the Midwest had been difficult enough without his calling me with another cheerless bit of news.

"I'd like to come out and pay you a visit," he said. "There are things I need to get off my chest."

He'd already said more in this paltry phone call than I'd heard him speak the entire time I was growing up. But the mere accumulation of words did nothing to advance my appreciation of what he was saying. Whatever was on his mind, or chest, I'd have preferred he left it there.

"Sure," I said, looking out the window at the river. "Whenever you like."

He told me recent turns in his life had gotten him thinking about a number of personal matters. The legal woes, he said, had only brought them forward. He said he'd decided to divest himself of all the belongings he didn't want or couldn't use anymore. Or that he thought should be passed on as a simple matter of inheritance. On this last note, he brought up the rifle he'd given me on my fourth birthday. A single shot, bolt-action .22 Winchester.

A vague picture of the rifle entered my head as he talked. In it, I was four years old, sitting on the living room sofa, clutching the weapon in my tight little fists, waiting for the flashbulb of his Argoflex camera to blind me. There was wrapping paper strewn over the cushions and a ribbon of undetermined color—blue, I suppose—dangling over the arm of the sofa. My mother was off in a doorway somewhere, out of frame, one small white hand pressed to her cheek, looking as if she were fighting off a toothache.

Four years old, and holding a rifle. I know. The image doesn't translate very well into this day and age, does it? But back then we were still living in the shadow of two wars, one past, one in progress, and firearms were a humdrum subject, devoid of the violent glamour they attract today. Where I grew up hunting was a right of passage, handed down father to son, like playing baseball or tinkering under the hood of the car. The occasion you chose to pass it down, if you were the father, was, as we say in today's vernacular, *fluid*, depending entirely on whatever paternal whims you happened to entertain.

My father taught upper-level high school English, and was regarded as something of a bookworm. He played chess, was an amateur botanist, and never went anywhere without his plein air watercolor kit packed behind the bench seat of his pickup. But he was raised poor in a rural community where men spent much of their time outdoors, and in those days hunting was, among other things, a way to put food on the table. So it was as natural for him to surprise me with that rifle as it would have been for him to give me a jackknife, or a bow and a quiver of arrows.

"Anyway," he said quietly, "I figured you'd like to have it back."

I assumed it was the rifle he was still mumbling about, and said, "Yes, certainly. Of course I'd like to have it back" though I didn't give a damn about the thing anymore.

He spoke in the same low-slung voice he used to use in the classroom in front of his students. There were long silences between the words as if he were parsing them out on a blackboard, making absolutely certain they were clear and unambiguous. Still, I felt he was keeping something from me.

Was he dying? Was that it? I had to remind myself he was eighty-three years old, and that, while he'd been in robust health his entire life, the years and miles eventually had their way with all of us. If *this* was *that*, if he was trying to tell me he was sick or dying or that he'd come to financial ruin battling some exotic virus, I wasn't ready to hear it. Nor would I be any *more* ready if he drove out and stood on my doorstep and delivered the news personally.

"I've booked a room at the Julienne," he said.

"You needn't do that. I've got room."

"I know you do." He paused, passing rather gracefully over the fact that I sounded relieved. "But I don't want you sleeping on your sofa. You've got a job. You need your rest."

"Sure," I said. "It's just that the area down by the river's not so good anymore."

"Well," he said, "It's got history with me. Your mom and I used to go to dances down there on Saturday nights. We ate our first anniversary dinner on a riverboat, you know."

"Yes," I said. "I know."

He inquired after the weather. He was living in Colorado now, and had been since July. He said the temperatures were still balmy there this time of year. It was cold and snowy in the mountains, he explained, but down below, in the foothills, folks were playing golf in short-sleeve shirts.

He talked on, and during the languid silences between sentences the .22 Winchester came back to me.

I shot my first squirrel with that rifle when I was five years old. Which now seems a lifetime ago. Or a different lifetime, anyway, when I still had two parents, a thick head of hair, and a happy childhood. The old man and I had gone hunting in the hills a few miles from home, and we were walking a slow-turning creek into the woods when he stopped and put his finger to his lips. I watched as he pulled his old wooden squirrel call from his game vest and tapped its bellows.

Aih-aih-aih!

My heart dropped into an excited crouch when a fat old fox squirrel answered back. I looked, and it appeared on a high branch in an oak twenty yards distant, chittering and flicking its tail.

The old man turned to me and nodded. "This one's yours, Conny."

He dropped to one knee and motioned me to rest the gun barrel on his shoulder. Which I did. I slipped the cartridge into the receiver and drove home the bolt and pulled back the cocking piece and aimed. When I did, I felt his breath go still along with mine.

He didn't move. Not even with the sharp pop of the report. His eyes remained on the squirrel the whole time, and we watched through the thin blue haze of rifle smoke as it scurried up the tree in panic and stretched out, prone, on a long branch as if to take cover from what it knew would not be the last of the assault.

"I missed," I said.

"No," he replied calmly. "No, you got him."

The rifle barrel was still resting on his shoulder. He didn't move. We waited, and after a long while the squirrel began to slip over the side of the limb. I thought surely it would fall, but it didn't. It caught itself at the last instant, like an actor in a Saturday matinee, and dangled precariously by a single claw, fifty feet above the ground.

I looked at my father. His eyes were fixed on the limb.

The squirrel hung there by that one claw and we said nothing.

I was certain it had died and become snagged on the bark, and I begged him to pick up his carbine and see if he could shoot it free from the limb. But he made no effort to do this. He simply waited, calmly, as was common for him to do when he wanted to will something into being, and in time the squirrel obliged —as I should have known it would—releasing its grip, falling limply through the air until it bounced dead in the leaves.

He turned to me and put his hand on my shoulder. There were no theatrics. No high-fives or fist-bumps or *I told you so* grins. Just the patient look of a man who'd learned long ago to trust the unerring clockwork of nature.

"I haven't lost you, have I?"

"No," I said, abruptly, moving the phone to my other ear. "I'm still here."

"I thought I lost you."

"No," I said. "I was listening, is all."

Silence met this remark. He cleared his throat and told me he expected to arrive in town sometime Friday afternoon. He was leaving Denver a few days early, he said, so he could drive the back roads and make stopovers in some of the small towns along the way and paint a landscape or two, weather permitting. He said he wanted to take me out to dinner at Diamond's, a supper club in East Dubuque, and asked if I would call ahead and make reservations. I told him I would. He said he looked forward to seeing me, and I returned the sentiment, though I admit I stretched the truth a little in doing so.

When we hung up, I looked out the kitchen window again at the lights shimmering down on the river. I'd always imagined that if you were shipwrecked on a desert island, or held prisoner in a concentration camp, my father would be the man whose side you'd never want to leave. Not because he was particularly genial, or optimistic, but because his remarkable calm cozened you into believing everything would turn out all right.

* * *

I don't know when my father's Quiet Man routine ceased being a comfort to mother, but I recalled a tiff they had that might have signaled the beginning of the end without my knowing it. I was ten, and we were sitting at the dinner table and she laid her fork and knife on her plate and announced—quite bluntly, and from what seemed out of nowhere—that she neither needed, nor wanted, the advice of a man who didn't know the first thing about a woman's body.

My father put down his coffee cup when she said this, his eyes scurrying around the table in a panic. Whether she was alluding to him when she made this remark, or Dr. Pickler, our family physician, or some obscure author whose work she may have just read, I didn't know. But whatever the reference (bits of which I rightly or wrongly recall being sprinkled with Latinisms) seemed to catch my father in a state of naked vulnerability. Mother may have been a housewife, but she was an educated housewife, and her moments of unexpected independence frequently surprised him. His cheeks grew a deep shade of red, and his eyes fell to blinking uncontrollably. He turned a glance my way and, drawing a sober breath, lifted his chin and suggested, pleasantly, that they take up the conversation later, after they'd retired to the bedroom.

But mother ignored him. She was determined to go on until she'd said everything she had to say, and nothing was going to stop her. We were in the middle of our meal and father's napkin was still in his lap, and I remember he picked it up and touched it to the corner of his mouth then lowered it, slowly, and dispatched it to the table with a subtle flick of his fingers. That was all it took. Mother stopped. She looked at him with the eyes of an obedient hunting dog, and lowered her head and said nothing more.

I think back to that evening sometimes, to the two of them sitting so formally in their chairs, and if I tinker with that moment, I can fix them. Fix *us*. If I allow myself to play with the clock in my imagination I can turn back the lost looks on their faces and, with an imaginary tap of the finger, nudge their marriage on course again.

Maybe if my father had done something other than drop his napkin on the table. Maybe if he'd stopped and listened to what mother had to say, or tendered a sympathetic nod, a thoughtful purse of the lips, they might still be together. Maybe if he had talked to her that night, husband to wife, equal to equal, their relationship might have saved itself. Come to balance in a new, healthier way. But it didn't happen because he couldn't leave well-enough alone. He had to have things his way. He had to lose his cool and commandeer the conversation with his silly show of power, pulling a napkin on her of all things, and backing her down with a ridiculous High Noon look in his eyes. Jesus. He had to get in the last word, didn't he? Even when the last word wasn't a word at all.

You let her walk away, I wanted to say. *You should have run after her.*

* * *

Mother relocated to Plano—*Illinois*, not Texas—where she moved in with an old friend, a woman she'd known since she was a girl. The two of them worked as tour guides for the Farnsworth House. Whether there was, or is, any romantic attachment between them, I don't know. Nor do I care. Mother did what she had to do, or at least what she thought she had to do in order to salvage what was left of her soul after half a century with father, and if it meant taking up with a woman, fine. That was her business, not mine.

What I objected to regarding their divorce was the timing. She and father were eighty years old, for Christ's sake. They'd been married almost sixty years, and the most rancorous disagreement I'd ever known them to have involved an embroidered square of linen. The whole affair was an embarrassment. Something that should never have happened. Or if it had to happen, should have happened a long, long time ago when they were young. People in rocking chairs don't walk out on one another. It isn't seemly.

* * *

"You got him through the heart," he said on the way home from the hunt that day. "That's why he took his time dying. It was a clean shot, but that doesn't always guarantee a quick kill. So now you know."

The pickup thumped down the road under the trees, over the washboard ruts, while the muffled crunch of gravel filled the cab and the late afternoon sun warmed me like a golden blanket. I remember waiting for him to tell me he was proud of me—

proud of the way I'd comported myself—but somehow, even at that age, I knew hell would freeze over first. My father was cut from the same backwoods cloth as his own father. They were hard, taciturn men, and both believed the best way to avoid saying anything stupid was to avoid saying anything at all.

We ate fricasseed squirrel for dinner, but what I didn't know was that the fat old nutter I'd dispatched with my .22 wasn't among the game meat on the platter my mother brought to the table that evening. The old man, it turned out, had kept my squirrel in his hunting pouch and later handed it over to his friend, Bill Clausen, a taxidermist, to have it stuffed and mounted as a Christmas present. I don't suppose mother had much say-so in that grim bit of sawdust and fur finding a permanent home on the fireplace mantle in the living room. But that's where it ended up and, to the best of my knowledge, where it lived until she and father divorced.

* * *

The Julienne was an eyesore of a hotel down by the river. Despite the best efforts of the town's economic development committee to see it razed, it still stood on the harbor, posed like a gaudy old streetwalker. I met him in the lobby at the concierge station, which had long since abandoned the frivolous notion of a concierge, and been converted into a three-sided wall rack stacked with pocket brochures featuring local attractions. He looked old and shrunken, slope shouldered with osteoporosis, and his hands trembled from Parkinson's disease. It would have taken the most accomplished liar in the world to make you believe this was a man who had engaged in felony assault, and yet, there he stood, guilty as charged.

We drove across the bridge into East Dubuque with the top down on my Mini Cooper. The night air was cool and fallish.

The river smelled wild and raw, and he tilted his head back and breathed it in with gusto, revived by whatever memories it stirred in his old grey mind.

Diamond's was busy with a lively Friday night crowd. A small jazz combo played on the raised stage at the front of the room. Our table was near a bank of windows that looked west across the river to the college on the hill where he and mother had pursued their undergraduate studies and where I now taught classes in cinematography and film technique. He wore a jacket and tie, and looked like something from an era long-gone—a sad anachronism of a man—and for the first time since I was a boy, I was embarrassed to be seen with him.

Our conversation was cordial in the beginning, father un-characteristically doing most of the talking. Waxing on about his days in college. He told me about people he knew and professors he admired, the drama department and the school's production of *Antigone* where he'd met my mother, who had, in his words, "inhabited" the role of Ismene.

He ordered a White Russian when the waiter came to our table, which surprised me, as I'd never seen him drink anything but scotch. I wondered if it was a sentimental choice, or part of the new *reinvented* Dad that had emerged from the chrysalis of their head-shaking divorce.

When the drink came, he took a single sip and set the glass aside. Then he changed the subject to that of the burglar.

"I caught him upstairs," he said. "He was stuffing my laptop into a pillow case he'd stripped from the bed."

He paused and took another sip of his drink. Set it down and, with a deep sigh, shook his head. He explained how he knew something was wrong when he walked through the front door and found the hall closet open. All of his coats had been tossed on the floor, he said. His umbrella, as well. It took his mind several seconds to comprehend what it was seeing, yet even then it never occurred to him that he might be standing in the middle of a crime scene. His rod caddy and fly vest were scattered on the floor along with a pair of rubber galoshes. My Little League mitt and baseball bat had been pitched on top of them. He'd picked up the bat, he said, without thinking. He said he harbored no intentions of any kind, except perhaps a vague desire to tidy the place up.

"We don't have to talk about this," I said, "if you don't want to."

He looked over with a small, dry smile. "No, no. I'm fine."

"Are you sure?"

He nodded and resumed the story.

"The pillowslip was filled with my belongings," he said. "And when he came at me with it, I— Well, I didn't deliberate. I just let go and swung."

"I would have done the same," I said. "Who could blame you?"

His brows arched. "Blame me?" He tilted his head to one side and pursed his lips. "No one, I suppose, if I'd left it at that. But I didn't. I'm ashamed to say it, Connor, but the troubling part was, once I'd begun hitting him, I couldn't stop."

I stared at this shrunken, gray-haired man sitting across from me. His house had been broken into, his privacy violated. His life threatened. "It was a matter of self-defense," I said. "You did what you had to do to protect yourself."

He shrugged. He seemed not to agree. But I insisted it was the burglar's own bad luck that he'd left the baseball bat on the floor, in plain sight. Otherwise he might have walked out of the place unscathed.

"Also, he's lucky you didn't shoot him," I added. "I expect you had the right. *Legally.*"

Father's lips pinched themselves into a flat, bloodless line, and a frown settled on his face. He touched the tablecloth with his finger and said nothing. The notion of harming another man with a firearm, even if the man were a miscreant, was anathema to him.

"When he came at me," he said, "I didn't know if he was going to attack or bolt for the door."

"How could you?"

"Yes, well. That's true. But the issue is, after I struck the first blow, I didn't particularly care."

I shook my head, unclear as to his meaning.

"I wanted to make a point," he said, picking up his fork only to put it down again. "And when I saw that I was succeeding in driving it home—that he was *getting* it—I kept on hitting him. Harder and harder." He looked up, eyes lit with contrition. Yet still the teacher. Still the believer in lessons. "It was as if a full stop wouldn't do," he said. "It was as if what I was trying to tell him could only be made clear with an exclamation point."

I saw him in my mind's eye, beating the man. Brutally, patiently.

"I hit him until I couldn't see his face anymore," he said. "Then I sat down and called the police."

I didn't know how to respond to this, so I said nothing at all. I just sat there.

He looked at me, grimly. "He's still in the ICU. But it's my understanding he'll live."

Our waiter returned and poured coffee, leaving a tall dessert menu on the table. Father picked it up and set it aside so it wouldn't obstruct our view of one another.

"I had to put Jenny down," he said.

I closed my eyes.

"The boy, the burglar, he'd abused her in some way."

"I'm sorry," I said.

He shook his head, meekly, as if there were nothing to be done about it.

Jenny, his bird dog, was an old, half-blind golden retriever. I had a photo of the two of them at home, in a shoebox somewhere. They were standing in the stubble of a cornfield on a clear fall afternoon, the old man cradling his Browning over-and-under in the crook of his arm, the dog at his feet, smiling.

"Yes, well," he said. "I don't know what he did, or why. But there was no helping her. She was a different dog after that day."

He picked up his coffee cup. It trembled in his hands. He set it down again and brought his napkin to his mouth and kept it there a long, difficult moment. The musicians were playing "They Say It's Wonderful" and as the singer swept her palm through the heavy air, he turned to the window, the river. I could see his face reflected in the polished glass, but tried not to look at it.

When he lowered the napkin and turned back to me, his expression was again untroubled. "Well," he said, clearing his throat, "What about you? Do you like your new job, Conny? The school? I'm sure the campus has changed since your mother and I were there. I should stop by on my way out of town and have a look. I probably wouldn't recognize the place."

"I'm getting along fine," I said, sounding less enthusiastic than I'd hoped. I was still fighting off the malaise that had come over me when I left the coast to move out here, still wondering whether I'd done the right thing taking a job in a place I could never love. "The people are interesting, I guess. The townies, I mean. The students are students, the same as everywhere else. But the natives, they're a different breed."

"Small town people can be hard to know."

I could taste the bitterness in my smile. "If it was worth getting to know them, I might make the effort. But the ones I've run into so far haven't provided much in the way of incentive."

He looked at me, tenderly, as if I needed forgiveness.

"Anyway," I said. "I've got some adjusting to do." I picked up my coffee cup. "The other professors and I joke about it. 'Culturally ignorant,' we like to say about them, 'and proud of it.'"

The music stopped. I glanced over and saw the band members laying their instruments in their cases. They were talking and smiling and stretching their arms. The drummer had risen from his stool and laid his sticks aside. He leaned and said something to the singer, who laughed and swatted his arm.

Father glanced their way, then looked back at me. "So," he said, pressing his fingers together. "Film studies." He offered a bemused shake of the head. "Who would have thought the world could change so much? College courses in the movies."

"Film," I corrected him.

"Yes. *Film.*"

I checked my wristwatch. The musicians had wandered toward the bar, on break, and it seemed as good a time as any to close the evening down. "Listen," I said, "It's late. You've had a long day driving, and you must be exhausted. I should probably get you back to the hotel."

He agreed, if only to appease me, and raised his finger, signaling the waiter for the check. He insisted on paying, and I let him. There would have been no point in arguing the matter, so I dispensed with any pantomime and directed the bill to his side of the table when it arrived. On our way out of the restaurant, we stopped at the cloakroom and collected our jackets. I could tell by the look on his face there was something more he wanted to tell me, but whatever it was, he kept it to himself. Shrugging on his coat, he followed me outside, down to the car, and we drove home across the bridge in silence. No further discussion of the burglary, or my job, or Mother.

* * *

We met for breakfast at the Village Inn on Dodge Street early the next morning. Afterward, I followed him across town to the 7-Eleven on Main, out near the highway, so he could fill up on gas before leaving town.

I parked the Mini in front of the convenience store and went inside while he wrestled with the hose at the pump station. When I came back out the Land Rover was still standing at the concrete island with the chrome nozzle sunk in its tank, but its driver's door was open and the old man nowhere to be seen. I turned and discovered him standing beside my car, waiting for me.

I handed him the smaller of the two cups I was carrying. "Coffee," I said. "For the road."

He thanked me.

It was a sunny morning and we stood admiring the sky, saying nothing. Each waiting for the other to initiate the inevitable goodbye. I stole a quick glance his way, and as I did it occurred to me, quite pointedly, or perhaps *disappointedly*, that we'd shared the most intimate moments of our lives in silence.

He reached over, suddenly, and seized my sleeve. "Look," he said, squeezing my arm, "it's been wonderful seeing you, Conny."

"You, too," I said, embarrassed.

"Thank you, again, for dinner last night."

"Don't thank *me*," I said. "*You* paid for it."

"You know what I mean."

"Yes. I know."

He glanced here and there, then looked up, eyes settling on mine. "I have something for you. In the car."

I'd forgotten about the .22.

"Don't let me leave without giving it to you."

I assured him I wouldn't.

We stood there, uncomfortably. Then he spoke again.

"Look, Conny—"

His brow tightened. I feared what he was about to tell me would take the shape of an apology, or an admission of guilt. An embarrassing tidbit about him and mother that would attempt to explain their inexplicable breakup. But what came, instead, was a confession.

"I don't know if you need to hear this as much as I need to say it," he said, releasing my arm and letting his hand drop, wearily, at his side. "But I love you ... and I need you in my life."

The proclamation, mundane as it might have seemed to anyone else on the planet, stunned me into silence. All I could do was look at him, mouth unhinged. Those words had traveled an entire lifetime to reach my ears, and now that they'd found me I didn't know what to do with them. It was as if I'd stepped onto a movie set where the director had just called action, and the clapper had clacked, and the cameraman was dollying in with his lens on the principles' faces looking for the money shot.

That was when it dawned on me. When I realized it wasn't the Winchester that was in his car, but the hideous stuffed squirrel that had sat on the fireplace mantle all those years.

I smiled, and as I did a pained look crossed his face. His eyes narrowed, and with no word of warning, he released his grip on his coffee and pressed his fingers to his chest. The paper cup fell, striking the pavement with a pop, spattering coffee on his penny loafers and the cuffs of his khakis. I reached out to take his arm but he brushed me aside and began staggering toward the Land Rover. Staggering, then running.

I wheeled and saw his shiny blue SUV rolling away from the gas pump with a stranger behind the wheel. A man I'd never laid eyes on ever before.

"You!" father shouted, sprinting after the vehicle. "Come back, you! Stop!"

As he cried out, I saw the carjacker's profile flash in the side mirror, his tattooed face breaking into a craven smile when he realized he was being pursued by a doddering old man.

I cast aside my coffee and started after them. They made for the exit, but a bread delivery truck rumbled into the lot from the opposite direction, thwarting the SUV's escape. The two vehicles nearly collided, but the Land Rover braked and swung left, narrowly avoiding the bread truck's bumper.

The scene devolved into mayhem. Horns blared, tires screeched. Screams and shouts rose out of nowhere, ringing in the air. But in the midst of it all, in the crazy-fantastic slow-motion chaos of the moment, my eighty-three-year-old-bookworm-of-a-father leapt up and grabbed the SUV's chrome luggage rail.

I stumbled to a halt and put my hands on my knees, raking the air for breath, certain the old man would be run under the Land Rover's wheels. But he hung on, somehow, even as the vehicle shifted into high gear and sped down the street.

His body flapped and twisted like a sail caught in a gust of wind. His legs churned, feet wildly treading air. One of his hands had lost its purchase on the luggage rail, but the other still gripped it.

Our eyes met, and I saw his face for the last time. He was wearing that solemn look of calm. The one that made you want to throw a book at him. Only this time there was something different in it. Something tender and forgiving.

Mama

BEATLE DARCY

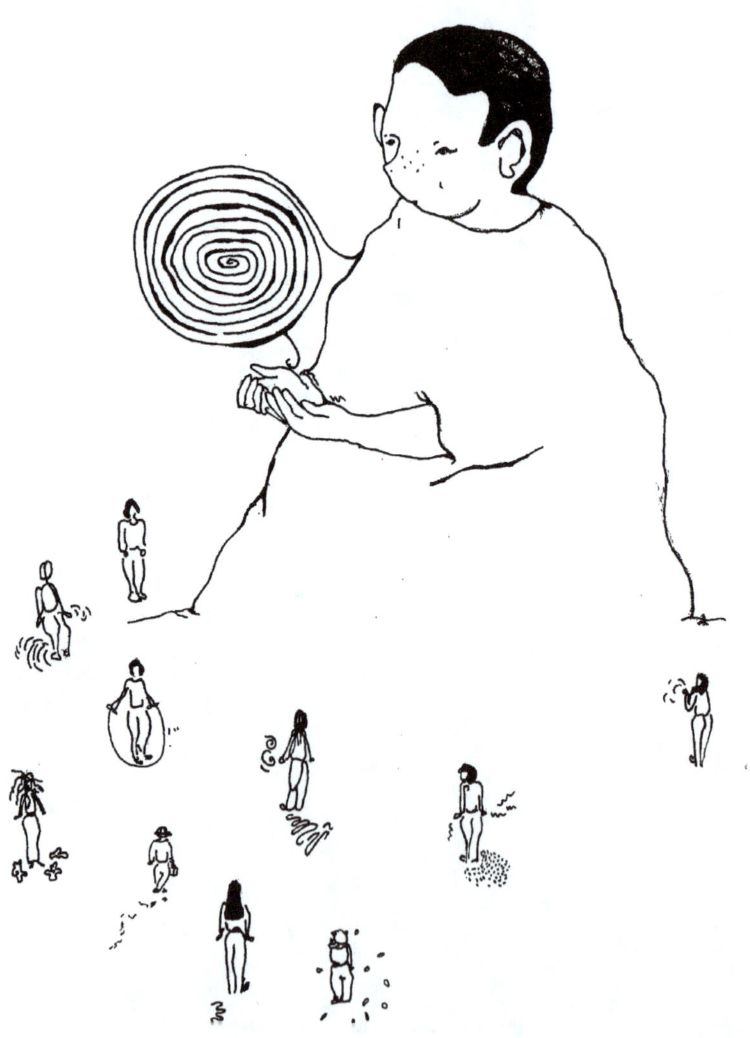

Mama, 2020 - Pen and Ink (8.5 x 11)
Beatle Darcy

Conversing with My Shirts

PETER SERCHUK

The shirts in my closet complain
they're too tired for work and yet constantly
this urging toward the next mirage.
In their pockets I find the yellowed lint of
previous seasons, old ambitions masquerading
as hunger and thirst. I explain that a mirage is
a fever that measures the distance between
need and desire, between the blindness of
what is and the blindness of what could be.
Unconvinced, each morning the shirts rattle
on their hangers; mistaking starch for resilience,
wrinkles for wisdom and a light switch
for a burning bush.

On Being Back In Some Saddle After Divorce

ZAHR K. SAID

They seated me, solo, between two couples, first-or-second-daters, full of nerves and vanity, electric with what they might unwrap in an hour or two. Headphones on, I kept the sound off, removing an earbud politely when I ordered.

Couple 1 talked as though they were laying bricks together. She was the mortar; the bricks were all his.

Couple 2 was mainly monologue: his job in the Valley; the long races with trademarked names, legal waivers; how he found himself running with a condom on an injured toe; how he hated to walk, *what was the point*? He wouldn't walk anywhere unless walking *with someone* to *somewhere, you know?*

She nodded, seemed on the verge of speaking; he remembered that she was a runner, *wasn't she a runner?*

"Good memory!" she said.

"Have you done any? Like the multi-day events?"

"No," she said, her shoulders curved forward with apology. "I'm more of, like, a jogger than a runner?"

Finding no traction on this topic, and perhaps out of material, he moved on.

The time there was this brown bacteria on his arm, picked up while smoking some cigarette in Cambodia—not cloves, not Mary Jane, something else you can only get over there. And the bacteria left these markings on his arm that even his mother— wait, he'd sent her a snap, hang on, it was on his phone, it was somewhere, it would be here, it was totally worth it... yes! *Check this out*—couldn't identify. The woman kept nodding until she saw the phone; no, she had never seen anything like it before.

I had forgotten the ritualized violence of courtship, the pummeling of small talk, the freedom some men feel to unload whatever, in anticipation, or signal, of pushing past and into you later.

I signaled for the check, unready for any of this.

Picnic in Coldwater Park

ANTHONY J. MOHR

Paul called out his bid—"Eighty cents!" In the spring of 1963, that was a lot of money for a pastrami on rye, even for a kid from Beverly Hills High School. Our student manual, *The Norman Guide*, pegged fifty cents as the "average daily minimum" cost of a lunch. But my friend wanted that sandwich. The girls had prepared our lunches and were auctioning them off, the proceeds going to "needy children."

Paul's eyes, a little small for his face, widened at the sight of that sandwich, and the moment he won, he said, "Hey, I live in Beverly Hills. I can afford it." He said it as a joke, and the remark made me smile. At the same time, it made me think of my father, who confessed to missing child support payments because "money's tight." Unlike my mother and me, my father did not live in Beverly Hills.

Paul didn't stop beaming until all thirty or forty of us sat down on our blankets and attacked our meals. We were reveling at the Squire-Adelphian picnic. Squires and Adelphians: the honor service clubs for freshmen and sophomore boys and girls. We held this frolic every spring in Coldwater Park, a cozy Eden in the far north of Beverly Hills, sheltered in all directions by a mile's worth of mansions.

With an ornamental stone fountain in the middle of the lawn, clipped hedges along the perimeter, and trees on the hills beyond, the place might have inspired a landscape painted by Poussin or Fragonard, two artists whose works Mr. Occhipinti required us to recognize.

Mr. Occhipinti taught modern history. He also was the faculty sponsor of the Squires. He had a narrow head, blinding white teeth, and hair as black as the suits he wore in class. That day, though, he'd shown up in sunglasses and a long-sleeve, button-down polo shirt that just missed being casual. Seated awkwardly on the edge of a blanket, he chatted with a small group of us clustered around him. We talked about nothing, meaning we talked about everything, with me listening more than talking. Someone said something about South Vietnam, but nobody was interested. We discussed our driver's tests (which I'd fail a month later), badminton at Richard's, playing Marco Polo in Gary's swimming pool, and hitchhiking to the beach. Would Larry, who was tall and tan, earn varsity letters in both water polo and swimming? Would Dick, a redhead with a patrician-looking face, letter in golf? Who'd join the summer session in France? When would Mr. Occhipinti start the unit on World War I?

"Next week," he said.

"That'll be fun," I said.

We drank Pepsi and Bubble Up. The crinkling of potato chip bags blended with the rustle of wax paper in which the Adelphians, as carefully as their mothers had taught them, had wrapped our lunches.

Many of these kids had known each other since kindergarten. I'd arrived in the sixth grade, thanks to my mother's remarriage, so I was still feeling like a newcomer, pudgy with more acne than most and a thicket of hair that was hard to comb. Someone told me the Squires had admitted me on the last ballot—another reason I didn't feel secure in this rarified group. But, at least today, everyone seemed to like me.

Judy asked about a musical work we had to recognize for "Culture Vulture," Mr. Occhipinti's two-week crash course in art, music, and literature. I knew the answer but was too shy to volunteer it. Randy—tall, with straight-A's in math—blurted out, "Debussy."

"It's Ravel, silly," his girlfriend Laurie said as she tossed a paper napkin at him. Then they both laughed.

Laurie was right: it was Ravel. That she knew the answer didn't surprise me. Laurie was brilliant—as well as the most fun-loving girl I knew.

After Laurie said Ravel's name, Susie, a member of the school's A Capella Choir, started humming a passage from *Le Tombeau de Couperin*, the Rigadoon movement. Ravel patterned it after a French folk dance from the 1600s, lively with jumping steps. My mother and stepfather had the LP in their record collection. I tried to whistle along, but, as usual, didn't whistle well. Nor could I sing.

Ravel had created the perfect soundtrack for our picnic, or so I thought. Half a century later, Timothy Judd, a music teacher and violinist with the Richmond Symphony, would observe that from its "bubbly opening" until its ending full of "jokes and surprises," *Le Tombeau de Couperin* "escapes into an almost childlike world of color and joyful, elegant ambivalence."

It was a day God made with teenagers in mind. A breeze that caressed. No smog to wreck our sky. An open, spacious field reserved for us alone. Randy and Laurie eased beyond the hedges and walked up a little hill, where they could disappear for a few minutes among the trees. He'd called me the morning after their fourth date.

"She kissed me," he said. "What a night!"

Another couple strolled along the walkways. I remained on the blankets, talking with the others and starting to feel comfortable. The picnic dimmed my usual worries about tests, the Cold War, the space race, and Martin Luther King in a Birmingham jail.

At bedtime, still glowing from the day, I put Ravel's suite on the hi-fi.

* * *

On Monday, Mr. Occhipinti devoted almost the full period to the western front. He wanted us to know the dead, who these soldiers were. British children with rosy cheeks, the same boys and girls who'd accompanied their mums to Fortnum's for their Christmas puddings. French kids who'd summered with their families in Vichy and Cap Ferrat. And German boys who'd learned to ride through the woods with the Hohenzollerns. Were these kids among us today, they'd belong to the Squires, just like us, and they'd bodysurf at Zuma Beach, just like us. But thanks to the reasons we were learning in class, they'd grow up to fix their bayonets, grip their rifles, and wait for the signal to go "over the top."

Mr. Occhipinti recited the statistics: almost ten million soldiers dead, along with ten million civilians. During the Battle of the Somme alone, there were 1,300,000 casualties—on both sides —which I found hard to stomach. Almost 58,000 killed on the first day. He described the trenches that snaked across the front—bodies in the mud, maggots on the bodies, blood, pus, flies, rats, piss, shit, puke. I learned a new disease: trench foot. I learned a new word: fetor—a strong, offensive smell. It came from the decomposing dead. And into this stink, generals hectored their troops with phrases like "hammer blows" and "the big push."

"If you were lucky, you lived a year," Mr. Occhipinti said in his mellifluous voice. "And if you were unlucky," he stepped away from the lectern, and I could swear he looked directly at every one of us, "you lived two years."

The class was almost over, but nobody moved. We sat there, in the middle of Beverly Hills High School, which covered over nineteen green acres bordering the back lot of Twentieth Century Fox. I glanced at the others. Mimi touched her mouth. Larry furrowed his brow. Laurie stole a glance at Randy; her face had lost its serenity, and her eyes seemed less blue than usual. Maybe she was imagining Randy's broken body snared in barbed wire. Paul liked to toss out a joke when the bell rang. That wouldn't happen today. Our teacher had made his point. I wondered how many Oxford students, graduates of the grandes écoles, and alumni of Heidelberg had screamed, "Mother! Maman! Mutti!" before dying in Flanders Fields. How many in our honors class would we lose in the next war, if there was one? Would anybody in our Modern History class live to write our generation's version of Robert Graves' *Good-Bye to All That*?

I wouldn't learn the understory in Ravel's piece for many years. He'd written *Le Tombeau de Couperin* to commemorate close friends he'd lost in World War I. Each movement carried the name of a dead man, except for the Rigadoon section, my favorite, which honored two dead men, childhood pals of the composer. How did Ravel react the moment he learned that, on their first day at the front, one shell had killed them both? I found it interesting—also logical—that Ravel made his suite light-hearted, rather than somber, because, as he explained, "The dead are sad enough, in their eternal silence."

Of Ravel's departed companions, one had been a musicologist; another, a painter. A third had transcribed Ravel's *Mother Goose* for a piano solo. They must have been bright, carefree lads, talented, like so many of the students I knew at Beverly. I like to think that we matched them in accomplishments. Paul would go on to receive four Emmy Award nominations; Bobby would become the dean at Yale Law. Carl would fence in the Olympics, and Ricky would win an Oscar. Patti would head a cancer research center; Dan would land a Pulitzer. Rich would become a Navy captain … and I'd become a judge.

"War is hell," Mr. Occhipinti said. The way he spoke—with such a calm, low voice—the phrase did not sound like a cliché. His words floated through the classroom.

The bell rang. Nobody talked as we closed our three-ring spiral notebooks, gathered our books, and left.

Kinetic Family Drawing

LAURA OHLMANN

I'm thirteen and the lights are dimmed—
clouds of incense permeate the small room.
Draw your family, this woman tells me.
She's trying to make me comfortable, with Mozart
playing in the background and Jolly Ranchers on the desk.
Every sense is accounted for, except touch.
I think of Mom's things, her dresser full
of photo albums, in the closet, outfits wrapped in plastic,
and her necklace laying inanimate against my throat.
I draw her stick figure first.
This action means that I feel the closest to her.
Dad sits in the hallway outside. Do I draw her hair?
It was gone when she died, but I draw the characteristic twirls.
Who's next? I hear Dad slapping
the ground with his foot. I put his body
next to Mom, but they don't touch. Distance tells us every-
     thing.
I redraw Mom's stick arm reaching towards him—they smile.
My sisters are next. I arrange their penciled bodies
on the opposite side of Mom. Twin curly-haired stuccato
     images,
but they don't have any mouths. Will she tell me what that
     means?

I've run out of room, so I draw myself in the bottom right
    corner
of the construction paper. She looks at the portrait and points
at Mom. Why did you draw her? I don't have an answer.
The ride home is quiet. Families throw frisbees in Markham
    park
and dance their tangled kite lines into the sky.
You're not over her, Dad tells me.
How do I get over her?
I never got over my mother's death, he says.
I look at him for the first time. The grooves implanted in
    his face,
the twenty pounds he gained and the wedding band still
    attached.
If I asked him to draw a picture of his family,
what would he show me?

In the Company of
Grief

MARY BUCHINGER

1.
One day I decide
I will teach Grief to talk

Grief wants to learn
the most expensive words
I pretend I don't know them

but Grief persists
        rummages through my pockets
        unclenches my hands
        raids my bank

and they spill out
each precious coin

the spending
knows no end

2.
I take Grief for a walk
fresh air stretch the legs
of course we get lost

at first everything is familiar
we have been here before
just like this hand in hand
but it grows dark and I don't
remember this street I've lost
track of where we turned
how long we've walked all
has grown strange the houses
vacant curtains pulled shut
no one to ask for direction

3.
Grief tells me
it wants to be a flower

Okay, I say, and hand Grief over
to a cup of dried-up daffodils

Grief climbs into the crisp
fringes of concentrated gold

the misshapen mouths
collapsed on themselves
petals splayed like flung coats

and Grief settles into the papery spathes
        sprung-open ladles empty
            no— filled with all that is not

Grief tells me it feels itself
known here

It's All Subjective

BRYAN STARCHMAN

A 10-minute play for 5 actors

* * *

Four actors sit across the stage in four identical chairs. They are simply named A, B, C, and D and the roles are flexible. The ARTIST speaks from the audience but can't be clearly seen in the dark. All four are being interviewed for some kind of documentary film but they are unaware of each other. It's as if the audience is watching each of their individual interviews spliced together.

* * *

A

"My name isn't Kate, so get off the bed and give me that green thing you're holding, the leak isn't going to fix itself."

ARTIST

Who said that?

A

My mother.

ARTIST

Would you mind saying it again?

A

(sighs, this is difficult)

My mother said...

(tearing up)

"My name isn't Kate, so get off the bed and give me that green thing you're holding, the leak isn't going to fix itself.

ARTIST

And that's when you knew.

A

That's when I knew.

ARTIST

That...?

A

That she had suffered a stroke. It was the beginning of something called "subcortical dementia".

ARTIST

That was the moment everything changed?

A

Yes

ARTIST

Thank you for telling your story.

> *A nods their head and exits the stage.*

B

It was October 15th.

C

A few days before Christmas.

(thinking)

1997. Yeah. It was '97 because I was 17.

D

The fourth of July, 2006. 4:15 p.m.

ARTIST

What year?

B

Oh, 2018.

ARTIST

And you got a call...

B

Right. I was still in bed. I drank way too much the night before.

C

Shooting hoops in the driveway when a patrol car pulled up.

D

At my friend Dwight's house. He has a pool and it was July, so it was hot. We were having a barbecue.

B

And my sister is on the line. My *sister*. You have to understand, we don't just pick up the phone and talk. So I knew something was wrong. And she says...

C

There's been an accident. And I'm thinking, shit. I bet that means the car is in the shop. And I'm pissed because I just got my license and I was supposed to meet up with some friends that night at the movies. But then the cop says: No. There's been a *fatal* accident. And I just remember my legs going. Like, the muscles and bones were gone. And suddenly I'm lying in the driveway.

D

So I've got a beer in one hand and a hot dog in the other and I have to sort of cradle my phone. I remember that right when he told me, Dwight's kids set off some fireworks. Like, way too close to people. Like a war zone.

(scoffs)

Like a war zone as I find out my brother was blown up in Afghanistan. An IED. Didn't matter that he was in an armored vehicle. Him and six others. Just gone. Just like that.

(beat)

I spilled my beer.

B

They found my nephew in the basement. With...a jump rope...tied around some pipes. 14 years old.

(tears up)

I knew he was bullied. I knew kids picked on him. He talked to me about it more than he would his mom, you know? I only saw him a few times a year, but he'd open up to me. He wanted to get into shape, so I showed him a few things. We'd go running together. I took him to DICK'S Sporting Goods and I bought him some weights and some shoes and...and that jump rope. *That* jump rope.

                                  C

Drunk driver. Two days before Christmas. Didn't even tap
the brakes. Just flew through the stoplight and in a split
second he made me an orphan.

(beat)

My dad...my dad was driving. And mom was reaching
behind her to help my little sister Phoebe in her car seat.
"Feebs" was always dropping her toys or something and
if I was in the car, I'd pick them up. But I was at home.
Shooting hoops.

(beat)

I told them I didn't want to go Christmas shopping. So
mom had to help my little sis. The cop said she didn't feel
a thing. Thank God for that.

                             ARTIST

And that was your moment?

                                  B

Sleeping off a hangover...

                                  C

Shooting hoops in my driveway...

                                  D

Eating a hot dog at a 4th of July pool party...

B,C,D

(together)

That was the moment everything changed.

ARTIST

Thank you.

B

Is that it?

C

Anything else?

D

What now?

ARTIST

Now you can go. The receptionist will confirm your mailing address and your check will arrive in two to four weeks.

(takes a pregnant, meaningful pause)

And just know that your story will help thousands of others whose lives also changed in a split second. Thank you for your courage.

A

What did you do with my recording?

ARTIST

Oh. Hello again. Remind me, your mother...she...

A

She had a stroke.

ARTIST

Right. I remember.

A

I would hope so. What did you do with my recording?

ARTIST

It's all part of a larger project, on grief. On reflection. Look-
ing back and realizing that our lives can change in a single
moment. I explained all this when you first signed up. Is
there a problem?

A

You're not a doctor, are you?

ARTIST

I most certainly am.

A

You're not a psychologist or a psychiatrist or even a therapist, are you?

ARTIST

(acting confused)

I never said I was.

A

But you never said you *weren't*.

Artist takes two chairs from the stack and sets them on the stage. Artist sits in one and gestures to the other.

ARTIST

Why don't you take a seat? I'd like to determine where this hostility is coming from.

A

I don't want to take a seat. I don't want to answer any more of your questions. I want *you* to answer *my* questions.

ARTIST

I'm an open book.

A

Bullshit! You said you were a doctor.

ARTIST

I am. I have my doctorate.

A

In what?

ARTIST

(eluding)

I am a lifelong learner and I've studied a multitude of subjects at--

A

I Googled you. You have a doctorate in media design. What even *is* that?

ARTIST

What is this about?

A

You lied to me. You lied to all of us.

ARTIST

Did you not receive your check?

A

What?

ARTIST

The $200 that we promised you for your story. For participating in our study. Did it not arrive in the mail?

A

It did.

ARTIST

And did you cash that check?

A

Yes, but that was before...

ARTIST

(standing)

Then I think we're done here.

A

(pulls a gun)

We're not done. Not even close.

ARTIST

(staring at the gun)

I think I'll sit back down.

A

I think you should.

There is a long awkward silence.
A is still pointing the gun directly at Artist but is start-
ing to tear up.

ARTIST

(searching)

I...

A

Stop!

(a long, shaky breath)

Just stop trying to manipulate me.

ARTIST

I am sorry if you feel you were misled by what we are doing
here but I assure you--

A

(cutting Artist off)

I went to the opening last night.

ARTIST

(realizing)

Oh.

                                  A

1500 art galleries in New York and my roommate chose the
one featuring...you.

                               ARTIST

I...I didn't see you.

                                  A

I made sure that you didn't. But I saw *you*. Telling people,
telling my friends about how *raw* your pieces were. How
you get to the very bones of your subjects. Is that what I
am to you a...a subject? Because as I recall you advertised
for "patients". Patients in need of emotional support.
Patients seeking help after surviving a trauma.

                               ARTIST

I don't want to get into an argument over labels. What
you perceived and what I was trying to offer--

                                  A

And there were no follow-ups. There were no group sessions
like you alluded to.

                               ARTIST

If you misconstrued--

                                  A

(pointing the gun closer to Artist's head)

Stop the bullshit! Stop it! I know what you did with my
interview. With *all* of the interviews. I saw it last night. My

face on a retro television from the 50s, telling about the worst moment of my life, over and over and over again. On a loop. Stacked next to a dozen other "subjects" on their own screens. A wall of misery. And for what? So you could stand around with your friends and talk about the human condition while drinking shitty champagne at $20 a glass?

ARTIST

(offended)

I personally selected that champagne.

A

It was piss!

ARTIST

Art is subjective. I'm sorry if you didn't care for it but I really need to...

Artist tries to get up and A gestures with the gun.

A

What? Get ready for your next project? How much are you paying for this one? You had quite a turnout last night. I imagine you could pay 250. Maybe even 300 bucks a pop.

ARTIST

(trying to appease A)

Would you...like to participate? Maybe that would be a way for you to find a sense of peace with your mother's passing. I'm assuming she's passed on?

A

Yes. She's dead. Otherwise, you wouldn't even consider me for your *next* project, would you?

ARTIST

(quietly)

No.

A

No. My story wouldn't really work for your next art installation if she was still alive and kicking. How did you explain it to my roommate last night? Oh yes.

(mocking Artist)

"Now that I have exploited the moment that life has been forever altered by tragedy, for my next piece I will focus on their loved ones' last words."

ARTIST

That is essentially the premise but you're missing some of the nuances that I--

A

What are *yours*?

ARTIST

Excuse me?

A

(cocking the gun)

What are *your* last words?

ARTIST

Really, this is getting a little melodramatic. Why don't you just put the gun away and--

A

You exploited the moment my life was forever altered by tragedy. You admitted *that* to my friends. You put my story on display for all to see. If you have such a love for this kind of so-called art, I imagine you're just *dying* to create your own personal piece. You should be thanking me. I have created the moment in *your* life where things have been forever altered--

ARTIST

We can discuss further compensation, if that's what this is about. Your piece was riveting. It's worth much more than--

A

And now...I want to hear your last words.

ARTIST

(struggling)

I don't know my last words.

A

That's the beauty of it. You can make them anything you want. But you need to make it quick. I'm losing my patience.

ARTIST

I...I can't even begin to...

A

Oh but you *can*. You have that luxury.

(beat)

My mother did not. She continued to have strokes. Dozens according to her doctors. And finally, her brain was so riddled with fissures and cracks that she didn't even know who she was. I got another phone call, after you recorded my story. What do you like to hear about it?

Artist doesn't respond.

A

I'll give you this one for free.   *(gets lost in the memory)*

Her doctor calls and tells me to hurry. She doesn't have much time left.

And so, as I hold my mother's hand and she looks at me...she starts to scream. Because I look like a stranger to her. A monster. And her last words aren't "Goodbye my baby" or "I will always love you". No. She doesn't have the luxury that you have. Her brain wouldn't let her choose to give me kindness and compassion and comfort in her final moments. You know what she said to me? You want to know what you could play on that *fucking* video wall of yours for everyone to watch and critique and analyze?

ARTIST

It's just art. I'm sorry you didn't like it. My work isn't for everyone. Maybe you just didn't *understand* it. If you'd give me a chance to *educate* you, I could help to make you see. I think the real issue here is that you feel guilty about not making more of the time you had *before* your mother got sick. If you had put in the time and effort while she was alive then--

A fires the gun. Artist collapses to one side, slides off the chair, and then lies broken on the stage.

A

She looked at me and said "You're such a muppet. No uniform is meant to have blobs on it. Now sing me a love song."

A carefully wipes their fingerprints off the gun, slides the pistol into the Artist's hand, and exits.

LIGHTS FADE.

Not Another
Takeout Tuesday

ROBERT BALL

Cascading red began to caulk the fractured windshield before I realized the world was upside down. People rarely left their homes as the sickness swept across the planet and slowed the momentum of summer to a crawl. For those who already struggled with the outside, global isolation was welcome company. Once a week, we were allowed out to purchase food and necessities. They said the scheduled commerce helped Earth keep spinning, so I tried.

Car rides had become a lonely affair. For fear of spreading the contagion, carpooling was strictly forbidden. My passenger seat had sat empty for ages, but it was nice to finally have a socially acceptable reason. I always took the backroads to my favorite pizza place long before the sickness began its reign, but all streets had become noticeably emptier than usual. Driving is a daunting challenge when there is nothing to focus on except your proximity to a violent death. With white knuckles and gritted teeth, I drove through the storm of anxieties trying to push into my mind. I missed distractions.

The pizza place was the last stronghold in a desolate row of former businesses. The comfort found in a slice proved to be more important than people realized; no one seemed to care about "things" anymore. As I walked through the neon glow amongst a sea of caution tape and undrawn curtains, I felt hopeful. If this business, these people, could persevere while so many others had given up, perhaps there was still a chance for me. Every time I walked in, there were normally greetings of the warmest smiles and smells one could imagine. Maybe I should have brushed my teeth that morning. Or maybe I should have changed out of those sweatpants I was wearing the last time I visited. Whatever the reason, that day was different.

A bell clanked against the door to announce my desire for inter-action. Conversing with others was never my forte, but the re-hearsed back-and-forth at this establishment was a script I had memorized and perfected: "Crazy times. It's the new normal. Glad you guys are open! See you again soon!" These repetitive lines, plus the newly installed Plexiglass separating everyone from myself, gave me the confidence I needed to make it in and out safely. But as the ringing of the bell died, not a single pair of eyes glanced in my direction. Panicked that I had missed my cue, I walked up to the glass partition. Not a word. Not a sound uttered was meant for me. Several glimpses finally came, but there was no consideration behind them. *What did I do wrong? How did I mess this up?* I nervously asked myself. The paranoia raced faster, and my breath grew visibly heavier as it fogged up the barrier between us. At the sight of the haze I had created, a voice yelled out, "Sir, back up!" My breath receded back into my lungs. How stupid of me. How completely foolish it was to think I could get close to people. The price was paid, and my order was shoved through a doggie-door. I took the box, looked back at no one, and retreated.

I drove away trying to contain my fervent thoughts. The only people I had connected with in months forgot I existed. *Every-one has bad days. They're just busy. Times are tough.* My mind tried its best to auto-correct as I turned onto the backroad home and pressed the accelerator. *You look disgusting. You probably have the disease. They know you always eat these pizzas alone.* The louder and more familiar voice in my head took over as the world began to hurl itself at me. The voice was right. It's always right. *They're tired of seeing you. Tired of serving you. People are dying while you shove all this shit in your face!?* My foot pressed down to the floor. The white lines in the road turned to bullets I struggled to dodge. There was not a car to be seen in either direction. My eyes shut. My lungs tightened. No one could help.

None of this is okay. Cut the wheel.

Voices stopped. Everything stopped. I didn't hear the screeching tires and couldn't smell the leaking fuel. My eyes fluttered open as if for the first time, as if my senses had been reset. An apprehensive breathe-in led to a strong breathe-out. I could breathe. I didn't care about what happened, I just breathed. I unfastened my seatbelt and spilled onto the shattered glass of my upturned car. Shards punctured my skin like a pincushion to let me know I was still here. My body began to tear as I dragged myself through the busted-out passenger window, but I was intact. For the moment, there were no intrusive thoughts berating my newly-refurbished perceptions. With one final thrust, my feet cleared the window, and I lay in the road beside the wreckage. I stared up at the sauce and meat that had splattered on the windshield and wondered how I avoided that same fate. *Please let me get better,* my mind pleaded.

After what seemed like hours, the sound of an approaching car restored my hearing. Flat on my back, I had been picking off shrapnel from the few remaining pieces of pizza I could reach. As footsteps approached, I shoved a bite in my mouth. Nothing had ever tasted more like life, and it had to be shared. A silhouette appeared in front of a dazzling sun and called out to me, "Sir, if you can hear me, help is coming!" In debt to my shadowy savior, I extended my slice of life to share. They instantly backed up to keep their distance and looked down at me with misgivings. Sauce fell from my outstretched hand onto my face. I squinted through the red covering my eyes and reached out the slice again in one final desperate gesture.

"Please try for me?"

Three Poems: The Bull, New England Morning, Marriage as Ecotone

TARA IACOBUCCI

The Bull

He is tethered, all
snap and bellow, afraid

    of release, no matter
    how prepared

for the sword, such spaces
left open

    for lashing. An imposing
    cape conceals a stabbing

truth: he will succumb
with or without a win.

    The bullfighter's calm,
    dark as a revenant, seals

the bull's slaughter. He is bred
but why does he still

    charge? He pretends
    it's like coming home.

New England Morning

This morning woe me with its coldest magic.
Outside my window, the generosity of snow

cloaks tree branches, amorphous flakes spill
from the sky, now blurred white. If I step

outside, it would smell colorless, taste of ice.
The world appears blank, disguised. Besides

the plow's tire marks on the road, there is no
evidence of morning's stirrings. If nothing

else, let us forbid the smudging of white
until the necessities beyond beckon. I hear

the wind rolling and this is all I know:
snow and wind and nihility and the swell

of numbness. I forget yesterday, its darkest
iris, my heart brimming with regret. Maybe

I too can wipe everything clean, start anew, cast
doubts far beneath snow piles, ignore

how eventually the temperature will rise. Only
snow is temporary, the unblemished crystals lie.

Marriage as Ecotone

There will always be tension: never smooth
mingling between two biomes. There is too much

of me, too many of my long hairs
in the drain. When you tell me to leave

the dishes uncleaned, that's unruly
in the pristine home I come from. There is too much

of you. Too many of your tiny fingernail clippings
in the sink. When our babies cried

themselves to sleep, you were not familiar
with this type of love. I am sorry

that I am late for every event, and you
are punctual—early even—unnerved

by wasted time. We argue
over the imbalance of our terrain

until one of us must give. When fresh
water meets salt, one has to yield

or float. If the tundra could meet
the rainforest, one must hold its breath.

The Accountants

ANNA MANTZARIS

The Accountants are talking about a potato.

One of them ate one. *You didn't!*

She did. But it was only half. More like a quarter. And no butter. And it was her birthday.

Salt?

A little.

That's not good!

I know.

The Accountants sauté their food in orange juice. They eat zoodles cooked in one spritz of coconut oil. They count out ten almonds and then put half back. They spreadsheet their meals and lunchtime workouts. They come back to the office sweaty and euphoric, pants sticking to their toned legs. *She really burned us today!* They say about the new instructor. *She kicked our asses! I'm only working out one more time today. Me too. Maybe two more times. Yeah, two more times and that's it!*

They go on fasts and cleanses and keep track of their co-workers lunches. The Accountants love to survey the Tupperware graveyard on Friday afternoons, approaching the discards on the lunch table before the containers hit the recycling bin. It's a "Who's Who of Who Ate What." *Laura had almost a whole container of pasta salad. No wonder she's huge! I spy remnants of a burger bun! Must have been Bob! Or Mackenzie. She eats like a big man! She is a big man!*

They go on silent retreats with no food. They plan girl's trips to places like Santa Barbara, arriving home puffy and regretful. *Steak au poivre. Coconut mousse cake. All those margaritas. Barf.*

The Accountants are keeping track.

The temp ate a Mounds bar.

The boss is off her diet. *Again.*

The annoying guy in Marketing had fries at his desk. *Like, we can't smell them?*

Someone ordered a burrito. *Delivered to the fifth floor, I think. A super with guac.*

One of them has a boyfriend, Meyers. *Meyers ate a hamburger at the game last night! Meyers' mother brought donuts to our house! Meyers eats so much sugar. Meyers thinks it's funny to eat ice cream in front of me!*

The other does not have a boyfriend. The other goes on dates and shows up on Monday mornings with written lists of everything they did wrong. She writes on post-its stolen from the office so she can scribble in the bathroom and shove them in her pockets. She fantasizes about eating a pint of Butterscotch Ripple naked in bed with Meyers.

The Accountants are writing a letter to HR. They don't think it's fair, *Let's say unconstitutional,* that there is an unhealthy daily snack. "Why do we have to watch people consume high-fat chips when we use our willpower to abstain?" they write as a closing and then revise before e-mailing, ending with "Thanks for your consideration in making our office a healthy, snack-free workplace for all." *Yes, that sounds good. Send.*

The daily snack stands. The Accountants fume. They go to the office kitchen to keep track of what's being served and who is consuming what. They mark on more post-its, bring them back to their desks, enter in shared Excel sheets, and save in folders on their desktops.

The Accountants start a petition against office birthday cakes. It passes. Or whatever a petition does. No more cakes. Somehow it happened. They lobbied like they were on The Hill. They ignore the glances from the others. The anger from the "November Babies" who were anticipating their chocolate ganache are seething, but *It's in everyone's best interest, no?*

The Accountants are tracking. On their phones. Their steps. Their calories. Their bowel movements. They convert the data into pie charts and graphs, then text one another. *I've got more steps than you! Yeah, but I had thirty calories less than you this week! I pooped three times on Saturday! I pooped four!*

The Accountants hate one another. At night, in their beds, one empty, one next to a snoring Meyers. They have the same fantasy. That the other one is getting fatter and fatter, blowing up like a parade balloon. *Pop!*

The Accountants are watching and tracking and talking about bathing suit season in January. *Seriously, it's coming up so soon. So soon.*

They are the grocery shoppers who take inventory of what's on the conveyor belt ahead of them. One of their glares literally sears a woman's head at Safeway when she buys a bag of chocolate chips and package of butter. The shopper goes to the emergency room for treatment, before returning home with a bandaged head, and baking her cookies.

The Accountants are here. In the office. And there. In your office. The Accountants are on the plane. They are sitting next to you at the restaurant where they order hot lemon water or maybe it's the truffle mac-and-cheese with a side of mashed potatoes this time and then go home for a cry to Meyers. Or no one or the cat or their mother or that goddamn neighbor who made the mistake of bringing over homemade macaroons. *Again.*

One of the Accountants is talented. She can paint. She works on an easel in her spare room every weekend. She's painting a Renaissance-like feast. It's *The Last Supper* meets *The Triumph of Bacchus.* People are round and big and fat and there are turkey legs and goblets and grapes. The people are rolling on the ground and falling off their chairs. They are smiling and laughing. The Accountant covers up the painting with a big white sheet at the end of each of her sessions. She remembers to double the sheet, for if you look close enough, through the thin layer of fabric, you'll see her face smack in the middle of a gluttonous meal.

Calendar Girl – January

TOBI ALFIER

The days are short, and sad.
Even the postman wears a headlamp

to deliver his satchel of nothing.
Light gray becomes dark gray

becomes night like a finger-snap.
Birds don't sing. Her chest aches

like the wildflowers pushing their way
through hardpan and snow.

Secrets course through everything.
There's nowhere to go.

No twilight. No graceful hour
to let the pins from your hair,

shake your mane into your lover's palm.
It's a casino with no clocks.

Only a watch to tell if it's morning
or night, and no matter—the sorrow

of no sun. She longs for the scent
of rosemary and blackberries,

the heat of summer, the length of days
—in the last warm move toward autumn.

The Note

ANNE RUDIG

I was nearing that in-between age—too old for babies and too young to be old—when we lived in a home on the best sledding hill in our midwestern neighborhood. With a backyard view of the wooded nature preserve that formed a boundary to our property, it was an idyllic spot for a boy of thirteen, a girl of ten, my husband, and me. We'd made it through their childhoods unscathed and were awaiting the thrills of adolescence.

Late one fall day, while the kids were still at school, I was folding laundry, trying to make our home look less deranged after I'd finished work and before everyone got home. Warm light spread across the kitchen table as a red fox slinked along our back patio and a barred owl perched in the pine tree. My thoughts of work relaxed into musings on missing socks, leftovers, and what to watch later. As I dug through an old desk, hoping to find a sewing kit for my son's torn shirt, I discovered a manila folder. Inside was an envelope addressed to me in handwriting I did not recognize. A photo with a note paper-clipped to one corner fell out. In the picture, a middle-aged woman stood next to me in front of a balconied hotel, like the ones in Western movies. Plump, curly-haired, and wearing a floral print dress, she'd greeted us when we checked in for our family vacation. My mother later said I liked to chat with her as we sat in rocking chairs on the wide porch. I am in my sleeveless yellow sunsuit, clutching Raggedy Ann, standing close enough to touch the woman's skirt. We both squint into the sun at the camera. I have no memory of this. I was three.

The note in the unfamiliar hand read, *Remember that being adopted doesn't mean you're not real. You're just as real as anyone else.*

I sat with the note in my lap, stunned, and glad to be alone in that kitchen. The laundry gave me something to do with my hands while I settled my mind. Not real? Had my mother told me that I was not her real child? I knew from a young age that I was adopted, but I must have buried the unreal part. I'm sure my mother meant well. I can imagine her struggling to explain the word "biological" and coming up with "not real" instead. It would have been important to her that I understood what I was, and what I was not. But I doubt she had the language for it. I could imagine sharing this information with the woman on the porch. Perhaps she'd asked about my family, making small talk with someone small.

As I stared at my fridge, plastered with my kids' photos and after-school schedules, the notion that I was not my parents' real child ricocheted inside of me until I recalled that for years it had confused me deeply. When I was young, I understood that there was something important that set me apart from the rest of my family. As I grew, I took that understanding out into the world and it set me apart from everyone else too. I wanted to tell people that I had a different last name, one easier to pronounce—but I didn't know what it was. I wondered, did any other child have this problem?

I felt a familiar hurt as I folded my laundry in the fading light. I guessed that being unreal had been why I dated my husband for eight years, afraid to be married. I told myself I wanted a career first. When I had the career, I still panicked whenever we talked marriage. I thought I didn't know how to be close to someone without scaring them away, but eventually I figured it out. I assumed we were too old to have kids, but they showed up anyway.

When our son was born, we were dazzled by his alert little face. For the first time in my life, I saw someone who looked like me, with my mouth and nose, my husband's round blue eyes. I was in love with him, but afraid. I felt unqualified to be his mother. When our daughter was born three years later, I felt ill-equipped again, but less so the second time around. She had delicate long legs and a shock of nearly black hair that the nurses decorated with pink ribbons. Also my almond-shaped brown eyes.

My children grew. I grew. I fumbled, but I managed.

Other mothers seemed to do everything so easily. I made cup-cakes, went to parent-teacher nights, sat on cold bleachers, and felt as though I wasn't getting it quite right. I worried that I would damage my children, that I didn't have the skills for motherhood. Perhaps I was an unreal mother too.

Our life was full, but like everyone's, not always easy. There were years when we searched the sofa cushions for change before taking our kids out for burgers. Elvis-themed birthday parties and *Blazing Saddles* sleepovers filled our weekends—there's something about the campfire bean scene that all nine-year-olds find irresistible. We juggled our careers so that one of us could be at the bus stop at 2:30 PM every day. We developed the ultimate neighborhood sledding hill by creating slick runs with hot water and trowels. When our children came in at dusk I sat on my husband's lap and we took the last run of the day down the icy track under a pink sky. We stayed married because we wanted to, because what we had was real.

This is what came to me as I sat with the note in my lap—I knew I'd made mistakes, but I did the best I knew how.

A sudden feeling unsettled me then, the certain knowledge that my parents would have said the same thing. At that moment, the kinship of fumbling parenthood made Mom and Dad more real to me than they'd ever been before.

I live in another house now, several states away from the one with the sledding hill. There's a different fox slinking across my yard and a red-tailed hawk hunts from our maple. The same old desk sits to my left. Our kids are grown and gone, but like most mothers, I've kept traces of them around. I look at the lumpy clay ladybug that squats in front of me on my writing table, sculpted by my son when he was four. It sits next to the oblong brown rock, painted by my daughter to resemble her guinea pig. With red lips, tiny black eyes, and curiously arched eyebrows, it snoozes on its side. Of all the gifts they've given me, becoming who they have become is the greatest of all. Now that I'm past that in-between age, heading for late life, I can see my children clearly and uncoil from the myths wound tight around me by my own childhood. I can relinquish the role of pretender, redeemed from the unreal.

The Evolution of the Stash

MCKENZIE ZALOPANY

Artist's Image Description

This is a one-page digital comic from my comic, "Slutty Cool Mom."

"The Evolution of the Stash," depicts the different places I hid my stash when I was an addict. Starting from beneath the mattress, to coat pockets, and eventually to my body becoming the stash.

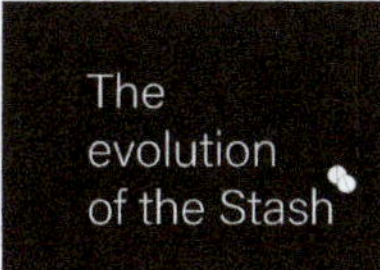

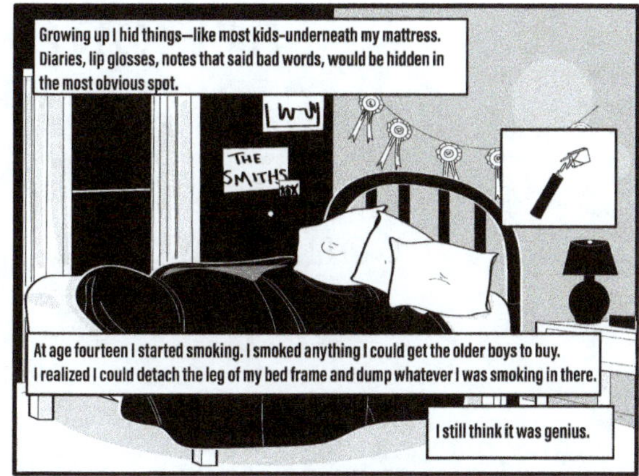

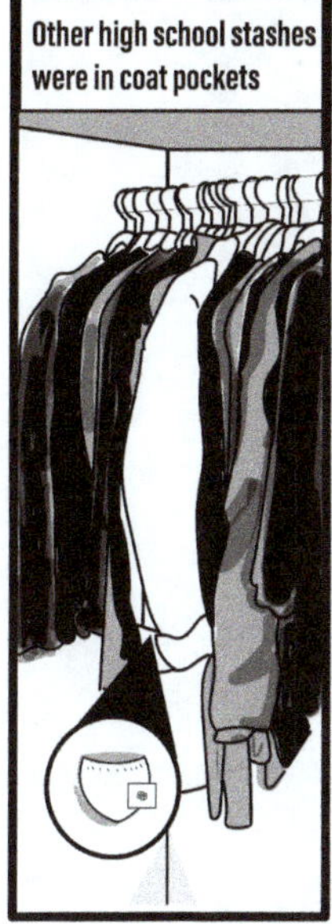

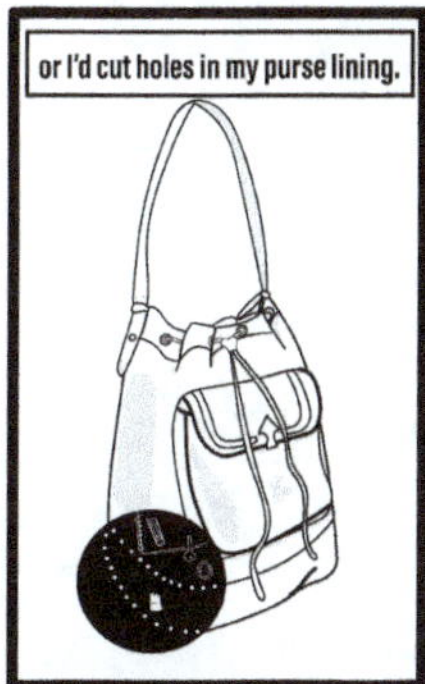

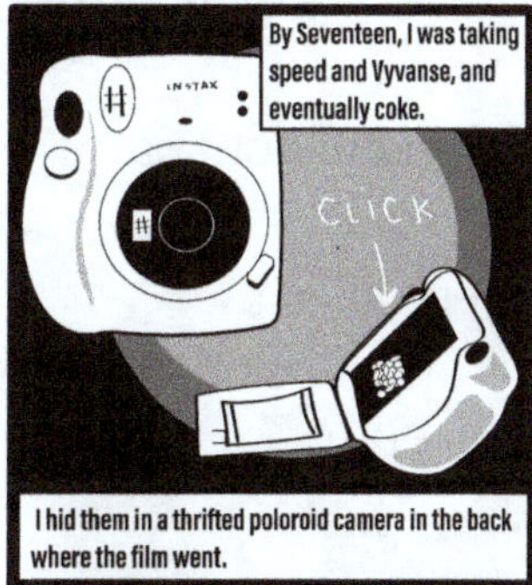

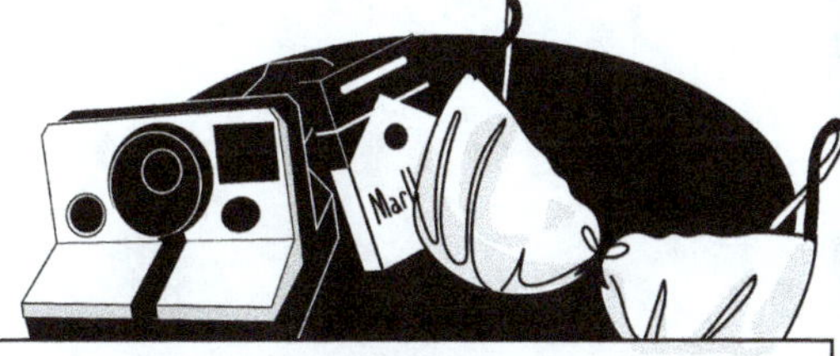

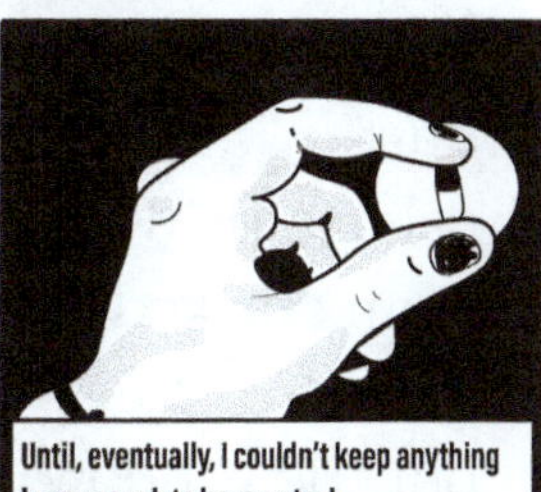

The Evolution of the Stash, 2021 - Digital Comic (1296 pt x 1728 pt)

McKenzie Zalopany

arizona

COURTNEY LEE HALL

i drive over cattle guard
over cattle guard

crushed chaparral

equalize i
am apart of the shadows
casted
on peaks

i am white, gray, brown
dust
caking, rising
from cracked palms

out the window
they drift driving
over river bed
over river bed stones

with it an echo
a coyotes kill
a finches song
the winds
kneeling
towards silence

i pull over to pause
pull over to witness
the barren
the fullness

i am a callus
a stone myself

brittlebush flowering
at my heels
cottonwoods
meeting clouds

Where All My Sick Things Go

LILIANA REHORN

The realization that I wasn't actually sick—at least not as sick as my mother told me I was—wasn't as liberating as I thought it would be, probably because I never completely believed it. So when Dad came to visit me in Cork, I found myself talking about how *not* depressed I was, how functional I was because X) I was in Ireland, Y) I was in yoga school, and Z) I would describe myself as happy.

There really is a difference between having a mental illness and being a writer, I told him while we were walking along Oliver Puckett Street, and he laughed. It was Sunday in summer. The sky was grey and bright and the streets swarmed with people. There was the sound of café doors opening and shutting, music playing on street corners.

We walked and walked and the rain didn't bother us. We walked around Camden Quay and circled back towards where I lived. We crossed the bridge near Rutland Street and the rain rippled the river. The air was neither clean nor dirty. It smelled like a hot kitchen with the door open, like soup and soapy water.

We talked about books. About what Alexei and Karenna were up to.

Near Douglas Street we saw a man collapsed on the sidewalk. He leaned with his back to the wall by the bridge. There were people crouched next to him trying to help. His face was contorted. It made me uncomfortable to watch something sad like that when there was nothing I could do. So I made it gone, and pointed out the gelato place down the road, and the organic shop where I would go to buy dates and Dutch peanut butter.

Further up the road, Dad said the gate at home's still broken. I thought of the gate and how the dog would stick her head through the gaping hole at the base, whining when we walked up the path to the door. And the front lawn where Alexei and I would play paddleball, the red brick wall where I would sit with Rico in the sun.

Thinking of all this did not conjure any sense of home. More than anything it evoked the feeling of an absence—one that allows you to think of things, but not feel them. Abstractly, I thought of Mom upstairs, sick in her room, the blinds cutting the yellow light, drawing stripes on the delicate clutter.

For the first time, we talked about Mom—how her illness had complicated everything from fixing the gate to moving houses. I told him that since leaving home no one else had made me doubt things that had happened or been said. I told him I was never sick and it felt good to tell him that. Stepping over a soda can, I said things were the way they were because she loved me too much. I wasn't what she wanted.

We crossed the bridge again, the water underneath tin-colored and swollen. We walked by taxis waiting at the curb, then circled back the way we had come. I thought what a terrible thing it was to love someone too much. And how when you get *sick* you lie in bed and feel your body hurt and watch people die on television.

We passed the spot where the man had collapsed, but he was gone. It had stopped raining. There was a stillness to the air now, the puddles of water like an aftermath.

Dad said she hasn't been well, but I knew that already.

When we said goodbye later that night, I walked home alone and stopped at my usual place by the bridge. The two swans were on the river again, glowing grey by the branches, the reflections from the street lamps drawing stripes in the water. One slept with its neck tucked in and the other just sat, and was still. I felt the absence in my stomach.

It was still there when I shut the door to my room. I sat on my bed, felt it turn over and grow. Now I wanted to remember. But it was strange—when I tried to picture my mother's face, I couldn't. It's not that I didn't remember—I just couldn't find it. It was like walking into a room with no light and touching whatever was closest—never the right things, never what you were looking for. I found the ghost of her jawline and the pale green veins in her hands. I found the things related to her— the black bedside table with its drawers full of chewing gum and chapstick, the Buddy Lee dolls on the shelves, the stacks of clothes on the bed—but I could not find her.

The absence was terrifying in its incompleteness because you don't forget, but you don't remember either. It's there but you can't see it, like looking at something after standing up too fast, most of it thick, black spots.

The absence exists because the thing that would otherwise occupy it is not practical to keep. Only sometimes does the thing resurface. It confronts you with the pieces. You remember some things but not all. And the more you look at it, the more it changes, the less certain you are of what it was.

I am sure of very little. Only the night that she slammed my bedroom door and said she didn't afterward. Vaguely, I can recall the day I died to her. I did not leave my room for eight days. Things swim detached—dust on the blinds and *I hate you*. I don't know what happened. Maybe I am *sick*, or was.

I haven't been able to see my mother's face in a long time. When I try I only hear the stairs. I see the doorway I would stand in sometimes when she was sleeping. I only half-remember things, like dead hummingbirds on the front porch, and getting pollen on my nose. I could write about home in a thousand different ways and never get it right. Just pieces of things like the sun on my neck and how heavy everything was —the leaves shaking at night, Rico on my lap, my Peter Rabbit light switch, transdermal patches that can make you sleep forever. And on my bookshelf rows of all my sick things: teeth in a box, my bad-dream monkey, my bones, my comb, my doll with the broken foot.

Five Windows

ROGER CAMP

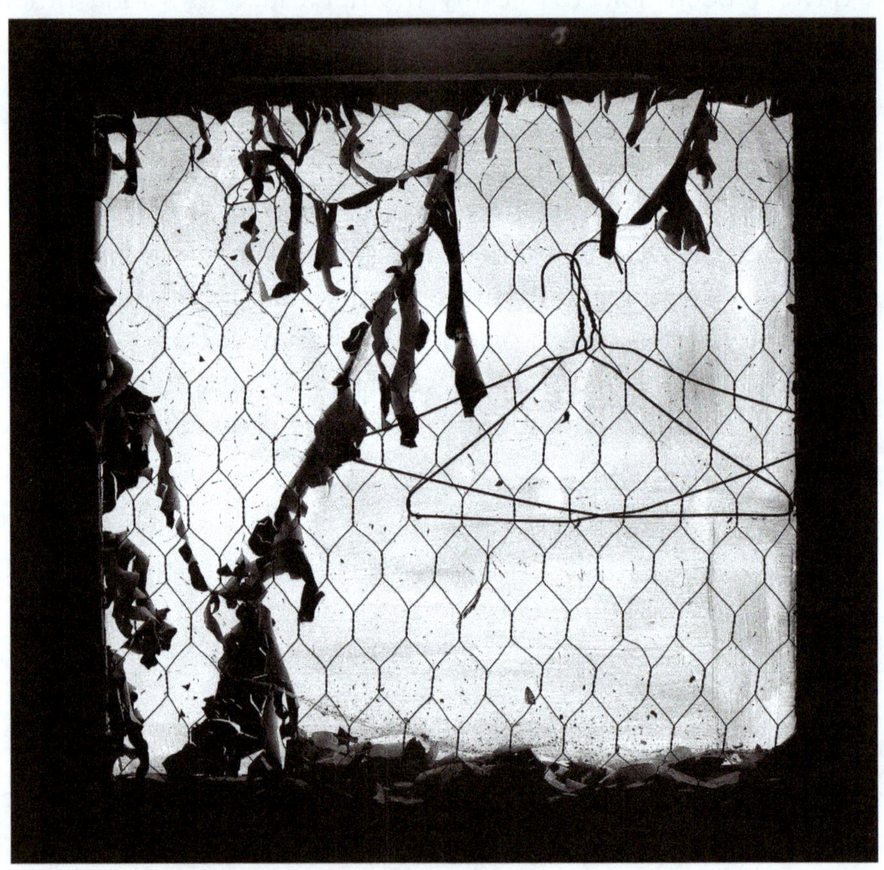

Screen Hangers Derby, from the Five Windows Collection,
1980s - Black and White Film Photograph (16x16)
Roger Camp

Two Poems: Atlantis and Man in the Moon

STEPHANIE LAMB

Atlantis

We met where dandelions grew
    from lion's teeth
And lilacs choked loving beasts
A place where angels
    sullenly clipped their wings
And demons traded in their howls
    and learned to sing
Pawns disguised as hubris Gods
Thrones of Kings and Queens
    adorned by false love
Crimson scorched earth below
 and violet tempest above
    You, me, them, us
Kingdoms fell and the ending re-wrote
All because the looking glass
    was cracked and sold
Ascension through sex and rum
And we call it immaculate conception
The sun shines bright
when the son is the most beloved
   Turn water to wine
   Bathe in the blood
Obliterated blasphemy
looking the fish in the eye
Escape on the wings of an angel
   But fish don't fly

Man in the Moon

I miss the nights the man in the moon would cradle me to sleep and the sandman would drip tangerine dreams into my kaleidoscope eyes. I would collapse tiptoeing from star to star chasing you. And with greedy lungs I would inhale tranquil skies and exhale hurricanes and fire. And I am sorry for that. I never chose to be a Chimera. I never chose to be a Chimera, just as you never chose to be a Phoenix with butterfly wings. We found ourselves drunk on poetry and our ocean minds were polluted with metaphors. But deeper into the abyss we dived, and never mind the depths because our glowing hearts always guided the way home. And home, home was you and me,... a crimson stained we. Tonight, I want to take a match to my kerosene-soaked dreams so I will not wake. So I do not curse the sun for another day without knowing how long until our souls share a moonlit dance under an indigo canopy of cheering supernovas again.

Summer Me, Winter Me

RICHARD FOUTS

On the eve of a new Millenia, a famous composer asks his opera-singer wife for the unimaginable.

Characters

CLAYTON SCOTT, Male, age 59
CARLA LEONI, Clayton's wife, age 59
RADIO ANNOUNCER, age 25-50.

Time and Place

New Year's Eve, 1999
The couple's Tiburon home

Running Time

9-10 minutes

CARLA
(offstage)

Clayton?

CLAYTON
(sits by a table covered with pharmacy pill vials)

I'm in the music room.

CARLA
(enters with a wine bottle)

I stole a bottle of champagne from the GALA committee. What can I get you? Do you need another pillow?

CLAYTON

How was your evening?

CARLA

I asked Michael for something to do so he let me play the triangle solo at the end of the second movement!

CLAYTON

Sweetheart, you're the most accomplished mezzo soprano of the 20th century, playing a tin can with the San Francisco symphony is hardly a suitable /

CARLA

And how was your evening? Did anyone of interest call?

CLAYTON

If you mean the president, yes, he called.

                              CARLA

And you apologized for your editorial?

                             CLAYTON

Where I said he has his head up his ass? I did not.

                              CARLA

Clayton, how about a New Year's resolution that you bury the
hatchet with the Clintons?

                             CLAYTON

He asked about you, by the way.

                              CARLA

Of course he did. I'm the nice one.

                        (in a Southern accent)

(CARLA cont.) I suppose he wants me to call him back?

                             CLAYTON
                      (waves a piece of paper)

He left you his private line.

                              CARLA

It's after 3am at Camp David. What say we call him right now?

                             CLAYTON
                      (hands CARLA his phone)

Suit yourself. He's on speed dial.

CARLA
(talks into the phone)

God, I hate voicemail. (pause) This is Carla Leoni. Please have
the president return my call at his convenience. Y'all, have the
number, **bitch.**

(hangs up the phone, horrified)

Clayton, did I just say bitch to the White House?

CLAYTON

Well, it wasn't me, at least not this time.

CARLA

Oh Lord, what if it leaks? Remember when Whoopi Goldberg
farted during that White House luncheon? That made CNN.

(telephone rings, CARLA answers)

This is Carla Leoni. Mr. President, how lovely. Yes, of course
I'll tell him. By the way, are we okay? You know, Y2K? Wonder-
ful. And to your lovely family as well. Yes, the dawn of a new
century. New possibilities! We have so much to look forward
to. Of course I'll tell him. Good night.

CLAYTON

That was quick. That Clinton motor mouth could send Satan
himself back to hell.

CARLA

He assumed we were apologizing for your editorial.

CLAYTON

Damn it, Carla.

CARLA

Relax. He said very nice things about you. Are you sure I can't make you more comfortable?

CLAYTON

I'M AS COMFORTABLE AS I'M GOING TO BE. Now can we please...

CARLA

Come on Clayton, it's New Year's Eve. Can't we just, look I'm sorry.

CLAYTON

No, sweetheart, I didn't mean to snap. God, I hate who I've become, how *we've* become.

CARLA

Honey, we haven't *become* anything. Have some champagne.

CLAYTON

I don't need champagne! What I need is to continue our conversation.

CARLA

Which was over before it began! Unless you want to discuss another bone marrow transplant?

CLAYTON

There's no second chance with this procedure. It's pass-fail and I failed. Miserably.

CARLA

Leukemia is such an asshole!

CLAYTON

Sweetheart, when I asked you to do something for me you said, of course, Clayton my love, anything.

CARLA
(grows angry)

Which did not include ending your life! You manipulated me!

CLAYTON

And you *betrayed me.*

(on CARLA'S look)

Sweetheart, I didn't mean that. Please /

CARLA

You know I would trade places with you in an instant. But pain has been a creative source for centuries, for artists not half as good as you.

CLAYTON

Not this time. I couldn't write a nursery rhyme let alone a symphony.

                            CARLA

But you re-invent old symphonic forms better than anyone.
You even do it in your sleep.

                            CLAYTON

Those are hallucinations from the drugs.

                            CARLA

Which is where I come in. You know how good I am at extend-
ing your musical vision.

                            CLAYTON

If I check out now, history records me as one of the century's
most important composers, not some hack who couldn't live
up to his last creation.

                            CARLA

Stop it.

                            CLAYTON

That my critics will dub "The Blood Symphony." By the way,
what's this about rescheduling your winter concert?

                            CARLA

You're too ill to travel, so I canceled it.

                            CLAYTON

You will do no such thing! I forbid it!

                              CARLA

Too late.

                            CLAYTON

Carla, I know that what you're doing, you're doing out of love,
I do. But sweetheart, you've got to think about

                              CARLA

Without you, I swear to God, I won't utter another note. You
don't think I'm serious, but I'm not kidding around. You can-
not tell me what I can -- and cannot do /

                            CLAYTON

You'll lose momentum that you may never recover.

                              CARLA

Screw momentum. Another year with you is worth any career.
Remember the terrible reviews I got for The Crucible? When
you took over, everything changed. Three standing ovations.

                            CLAYTON

The orchestra was covering you, and the percussion was all
wrong. Once I reengineered the sound it was all you. That, and
my threat to burn the Seattle Symphony to the ground. Works
every time!

                              CARLA

(both laugh)

Even your laugh is music. I've missed it.

(with anger)

Now, why won't you let go of this insane idea?

                    CLAYTON

Because I love you. And, because you love me.

                    CARLA

Quoting your wedding vows. That's not fair.

                    CLAYTON

You plagiarized your vows, that wasn't fair either.

                    CARLA

Hey, no one said they had to be original.

                    CLAYTON
               (quoting CARLA's vows)

Summer me, winter me.

                    CARLA

And with your kisses morning me, evening me.

                    CLAYTON

And as the world slips far away, star away,

                    CARLA

Forever me with love.

CLAYTON

I thought it was from Camelot. Seemed like something Guine-
vere would have said to Lancelot.

CARLA

Forgive me, my prince?

CLAYTON

Of course. Even if you, my darling, came off as the Poet Laure-
ate, while I came off as a...

CARLA

Man in love. When you recited your simple, boyish vows I
remember thinking "I'ver never felt so loved."

CLAYTON

And I remember thinking, did she just quote Rogers and fuck-
ing Hammerstein?

CARLA
(both laugh)

If I drown you in memories, it will distract you from the pain,
help you remember all the reasons.

CLAYTON

You'll eventually run out of stories.

CARLA

Goddamnit Clayton, I'll re-invent them so you won't get bored.
Just trust me for once.

CLAYTON

You could never bore me. And I've always trusted you.

CARLA

Then stop cornering me! Dismissing me! Clayton, consider the enormity of what you're asking.

CLAYTON

If you really love me.

CARLA

I will NOT entertain the rest of that sentence. These traps you set, they're cruel and underhanded.

CLAYTON

That's not what I .... Carla, you know I've never been one for hidden agendas.

CARLA
(pauses, then starts to cry)

And you've always been there for me. So why can't I be here now, for you?

CLAYTON

But, you can.

CARLA
(exasperated)

Oh my God, you're doing it again!

CLAYTON

Sweetheart, this is for both of us. If you'll just reconsider how...

CARLA

Reconsider? RECONSIDER? All right, you win! Is that what you fucking need to hear? That it's Game Over? And I shouldn't be such a sore loser?

CLAYTON

You and I have never been competitors.

CARLA

Which is why I fell in love with you. But now, you've turned us into negotiators!

CLAYTON

No, Carla. That's not.

CARLA

Except it's your way or the highway. Clayton, if you really think you're doing this for me, for us, there's only one way I will ever agree to it. And I swear to God -- it's absolutely non-negotiable.

CLAYTON

Then forever me with love.

Lights fade as Frank Sinatra's
Summer Me, Winter Me comes up.

Our first story of the year 2000 is a sad one. Composer Clayton Scott, and his opera-singer wife, Carla Leoni, were found dead this morning in what police are calling a double suicide. We're still gathering the details, but for now, Clayton Scott and his wife Carla -- found dead in their San Francisco home. They were 59.

Photographs

GLORIA KEELEY

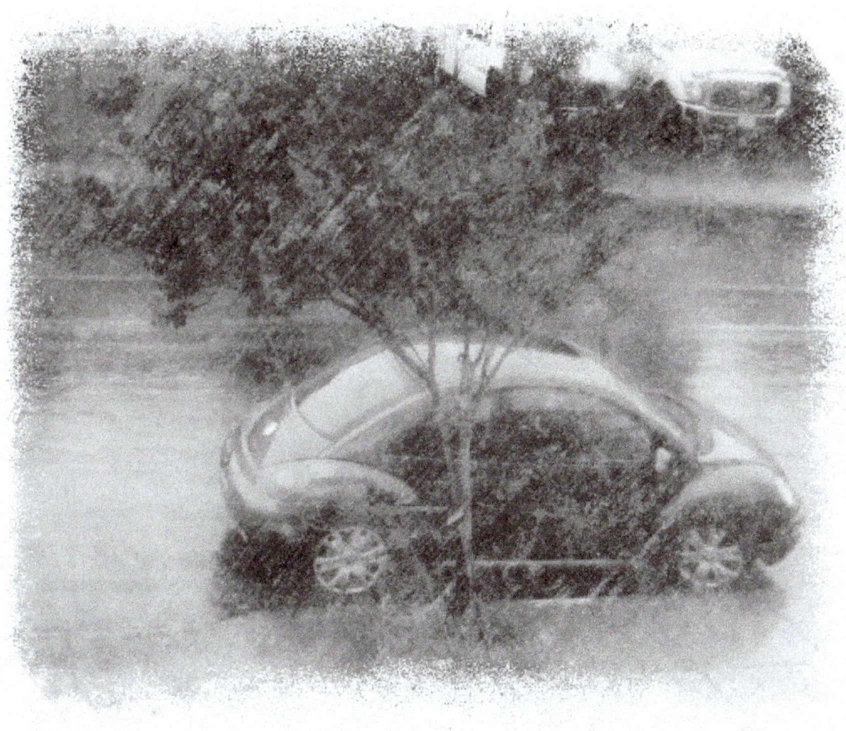

Bug in Rain - Black & White Photograph
Gloria Keeley

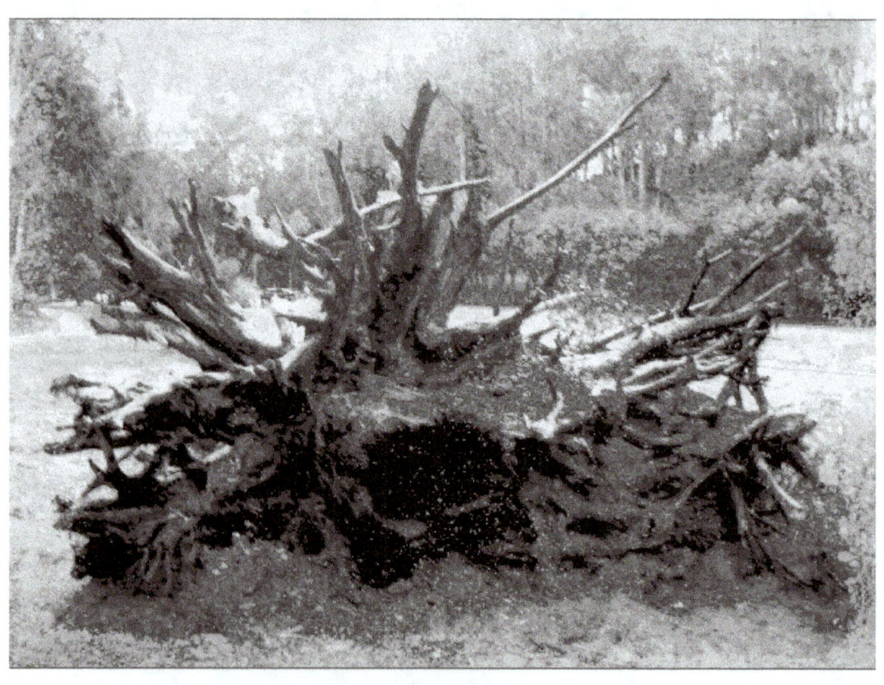

Uprooted - Digital Photograph
Gloria Keely

"I Have Eaten One of Every Type of Bird in This Forest," Said the Ornithologist

HOLLY DAY

He opens the wings of the bird over the nest
poses her protectively around the clutch. At the last minute
he rearranges the eggs so that the ends all point
toward one another, instead of lying haphazardly in the basin
    of leaves and twigs
as they did when he first found his subject.

The little bird's head lolls to one side, glassy eye stares back
up at nothing. Sighing, the ornithologist picks up the little body
sets it back down in the nest, restores the maternal pose,
props the head up with a bit of straw
against her neck, where it can't be seen. She could be alive now
a tiny blue-green finch, patiently shading her brood
against her breast, under her outspread wings.

He fills out his sketch with a backdrop of greenery
surrounds his prey in platitudes, a vision of some place un-
    touched
by the fans of his books.

Poor, Stupid Thing

R. E. SAWYER

Clara sits on the living room floor, staring at the blank television screen and wondering how she's supposed to feel about her dead husband. Sad, of course. And she does feel that, but there's something else. Something she can't quite face.

As she takes a sip of her coffee, wincing at the cold sourness on her tongue, her phone vibrates in her lap.

Chris has texted, *Want me to bring by dinner after work?*

Merely tolerable as her husband's best friend when Dean was alive, Chris has been helpful in an uncharacteristically unobtrusive way in the weeks since the funeral. It's only now Clara realizes she hadn't really known Chris before. He was always around, but Clara thought of him more like a loud, obnoxious puppy that belongs to someone else rather than as a person to have an actual conversation with. And yet, where everyone else has disappeared from her life, Chris makes the time to check-in.

Sure, she texts back.

Preferences?

Clara wonders if Chris will bring Maddie, the only positive consequence of a hard and fast Tinder relationship that dissolved before the kid was even born. Maddie's got these cute little ringlets and big brown eyes that Clara hopes she'll grow into. He gets her every other weekend but hasn't brought her around lately. He's good with her, but Clara thinks he doesn't know what to do with himself most of the time.

Whatever, she replies.

* * *

After wandering around the darkened house for most of the morning, unsure of what she's supposed to need or want, Clara steps into the bedroom she used to share with Dean. She's conscious of her light step, never pounding through the house like she used to do when Dean would jokingly—but in that way that makes you think it's less a loving tease and more annoyed scolding—tell her she sounded like an elephant tromping up and down the stairs. Now that it's only her, she's afraid she might miss something underneath the everyday vibrations of the house if she makes too much noise.

Clara once told Dean that if she died before he did, she'd come back to haunt him. Make sure there weren't any hussies encroaching on her territory in his time of need. Dean had rolled his eyes and said if he died first, he'd choose not to bother her, ethereally or otherwise. Sometimes she hopes he didn't get a choice.

Clara sits down on her side of the lumpy, yard-sale mattress where the red satin fitted sheet has come loose. It's all so much shit under a glitzy veneer. All of it. She picks up her heavy pillow—a silly thing filled with buckwheat that Dean saw on tv and thought it would help with her snoring—and smooths her fingertips across the enclosed husks. Her jaw clenches involuntarily, and she feels the burn behind her eyes as she brings the pillow to her face and begins to scream.

Into the dampening black satin that has sucked into her mouth, Clara screams to banish the tears she's so very tired of wiping from the dried-out, puffed-up skin of her cheeks. She read somewhere that this is cathartic for people experiencing grief, so she tries to work up a real blood curdler like in all the best B-horror movies. All she manages is a pathetic, guttural keening. When her gritty smoker's lungs finally send up a series of scratchy, iron-tasting coughs, Clara imagines herself being strangled. She doesn't feel any sort of relief. She wants a cigarette, though she hasn't smoked since Dean died because he'd always nagged her about it when he was alive.

She feels stupid and self-conscious, though there's no one around to hear her. She can't stop imagining she's not really alone in their house. *Her* house. She can't stop thinking plurally; she doesn't know how to be an *I*. And she doesn't know what to do with her anger and fear and sadness because the comfort that comes with being an *us*, is gone.

Unless you count the cat.

The chubby orange tabby had darted from the room when the screaming started. Now, in that same kind of piercing silence left in the aftermath of an eruption, the cat jumps back onto the bed and stretches his neck to sniff at Clara from a safe distance. Clara wraps one arm around the pillow, clutching it to her chest, and with the other, lifts a trembling palm to his nose. The cat accepts this apology and allows her to smooth the raised fur on his back.

"That's a poofy tail you have," Clara says, trying for the same cooing tone Dean would use when the cat would spook at his own shadow. He stares at her for a moment before flopping onto Dean's pillow, where he begins his methodical bathing ritual.

The cat's name is Daryl, but Clara doesn't call him that. If she's feeling affectionate, she calls him little dude or buddy. Mostly she sticks to calling him cat. She's never cared for cats. She thinks they're weird and judgmental. She'd thought Dean had known that, but after he'd given the cat the kind of name you'd give a human baby and started carrying him around the house, murmuring, "Who's my sweet little man?" she hadn't wanted to hurt his feelings. He'd gotten the cat for her, after all.

Sometime after their first date in the karaoke bar across from the university campus, but before their engagement junior year, they'd agreed: no children. Or, Dean had decided, and Clara's silence had been taken as agreement.

Dean claimed he didn't see the point in having children, but Clara suspected he was afraid of turning into his mostly absent, always-drunk father. She hadn't been the kind of girl who dreamt of a hoard of kids running around a blissfully chaotic home, but she'd never been altogether against it, either. She'd figured, if it happened, it happened. Leave it to fate and all that.

It was Dean who'd made up her mind to rattle off all the reasons she definitely did not want kids whenever the subject was brought up. Once, when her mother asked for what felt like the hundredth time in the span of a week whether Clara was ever going to give her a grandchild, Clara snapped, "I don't want a kid in the same way you don't want shit in your water heater." She hadn't even known what she'd meant by that. Her mother's persistence was like a chronic burning in Clara's chest. A pain that words alone couldn't cure no matter how hard she tried. Eventually, she'd given up explaining altogether, and whenever the baby question came up, she'd announce, "My body, my choice!" and walk out of the room.

She'd thought she could make herself believe all this. She *had* believed it. But two years ago, as Dean was finishing his MBA and preparing to take over his uncle's pet store—specializing in luxe toys, gaudy outfits, and gourmet foods (all of which Clara thought excessive and sure to not bring them continued financial stability)—Clara felt that something was missing. That they could use something else to love. She didn't say this to Dean. His mother, having ignored the lump in her breast until it was too late, had died around the same time, and Clara hadn't found the words to renegotiate the issue of children.

When Dean presented her with a scraggly, mewling, three-month-old kitten the day after his graduation, she'd taken it as a sign that there would be no renegotiation. Though the kitten was his gift to her for supporting him through grad school, the damn thing promptly chose Dean as Lord and Savior of Felines. She tried to love it. Despite her attempts at bribery and what felt like constant playing and grooming, the little shit would curl up on Dean's chest every night as they settled into bed and swat Clara's hands away when she tried to cuddle up with them.

She's still trying to love the cat, who is now purring as he licks and chews at the pads of his front paws, the unexpected break in his perfectly silent afternoon nap forgotten.

"Hey cat," Clara says. "I guess I'm stuck with you." He pauses long enough to give her a slow blink. "Poor, stupid thing," she says.

* * *

Clara wakes sometime later, her tank top twisted, the bottoms of her sweatpants bunched up around her knees. She doesn't remember falling asleep; she does that a lot lately. She squints at the bright edge around the gray blackout curtains and assumes it's afternoon. The cat is gone again, holed up somewhere less restless.

Struggling upright, she swipes at the matted hair on her face and neck with one hand while pulling the greasy tank away from her chest and stomach with the other. Her head is pounding, her tongue thick and furry like she'd been sucking on antibiotics. She knows she's dehydrated. The sink in the master bathroom is right there, but she thinks of taking care of herself as a kind of betrayal.

Glaring at the thought of her own emotional instability, she grabs the pillow from Dean's side of the bed and crashes back down. She doesn't even know what she's grieving for anymore.

* * *

Although her parents have upgraded to motoring around in an RV and living part-time in a small, stylish bungalow in Puerto Vallarta, they used to be avid—albeit amateur—campers, dragging Clara and her sister Mallory all over the southwestern United States and on up through the Pacific Northwest. They were never particularly outdoorsy in the hike every weekend and sleep directly under the stars kind of way. They didn't hunt, but once in a while, someone would catch a fish. Her father could build a decent fire as long as there was enough leftover newspaper and lighter fluid. Her mother refused to camp anywhere that lacked a body of water deep enough to swim in, lest she becomes inconsolably bored. Clara and Mal—younger than Clara by two years—fancied themselves explorer-scientists, sneaking home specimens of rock or bone or live insects which they were sure no one else in the whole world had ever discovered before.

It's one of these family trips that serve as the basis for Clara's recurring dream, which started the night Dean gifted her the cat. At least once a week, the entire experience plays out in her subconscious and, despite the experience having a happy ending in her memory, dreams have a funny way of twisting reality.

In her memory of the event, ten-year-old Clara and her family are camping on the beach of some small lake in a rocky, wooded area in California or Nevada or Wyoming. Mal wants to splash around in the water, and their mother is dipping bright orange floaties into the lake so she can tug them up to Mal's armpits, even though she knows how to swim. This is where the dream always starts.

Clara doesn't want to swim; she wants to explore. She stamps her feet and tries to coax her sister out of the water, but Mal starts up that high-pitched whine that has always irritated their mother.

"Chrissake, Clara, leave her alone," their mother says as she towels off her legs and feet. She looks down the beach to the girls' father, who is fishing, sitting in a woven folding chair with the pole propped in the sand in front of him, and paying attention to nothing but the beer can in his lap. Their mother sighs and says, "Just watch your sister, okay. I'm taking a nap."

Clara tries to tell her mother it isn't fair, but her mother ignores her as she unzips the bright red four-person tent and disappears inside.

Mal laughs, but not in a malicious way. Later, she will tell Clara how sorry she is and that they should have gone exploring together and she will never, ever let Clara go by herself again. But right now, in the dream, she's only playing, leaping up out of the water, swinging her arms toward Clara, who stands with her arms crossed, glaring at her little sister. The splash soaks

Clara's boots and the tops of her socks, and she gasps, taking an exaggerated leap backward.

"You can watch your damn stupid self," Clara shouts.

'Damn' is the worst swear she's ever said in her parents' hearing, and she isn't supposed to call her sister 'stupid' anymore. She storms off toward the trail they'd walked the day before, shaking, and sure one or both of her parents will be right behind her to swat her butt and demand an apology. But they don't come after her, and Clara keeps walking.

When she feels the first few drops of rain on her head and shoulders and turns around to run back to camp, she realizes she's gone off the trail. She'd been muttering to herself about how mean and stupid everyone was, stomping through the trees, paying no attention to where she was going or to the sounds of the woods. As she spins around, searching for the clearly marked path back to her family, she understands how alone she is and how loud the air is with the rustling of leaves and growing rain and whatever else might be out here watching her.

Clara doesn't think to call out. She runs with her arms outstretched, slapping away low-hanging branches that poke and scrape. She slips only once when the rumblings of distant thunder cause her to lose her footing and tumble into a dry creek bed. She stands, shaking in her wet clothes, and totters to a low overhang that shields her from the rain. As she crouches to check her scraped knees, she begins to cry, believing she will never, ever be found.

In her memory of this event, Clara is soon stirred by her father's frantic and excited shouts of, "I've got her! I've got her!" She'd been gone a little over an hour when her mother emerged from the tent and realized her oldest daughter was gone. Once she is brought back to camp, she keeps her eyes down, pressing a finger into the hard lump of a mosquito bite on the inside of her elbow while her parents lecture her on the perils of being a child in the woods alone and warn her to never, ever do that to them again.

In her dream, though, she is never brought back to camp. Never reunited with her family. Never saved. In her dream, as Clara stands to run toward the sound of her father's voice, she doesn't recognize the body she inhabits as her own; it is not the body of a scrawny ten-year-old girl, but the tired, misused body of a woman. Her father's cries draw closer, but the sound of his voice, too, is wrong. It's a voice she knows, but one that doesn't belong here. It is Dean's voice.

His tone is a menacing coolness that slithers down her spine. She crawls back under the overhang, her hand clamped over her mouth. She's not afraid *of* him, she realizes. She's afraid of *being seen* by him.

Every time this dream recurs, it is at this moment of aware-ness when Clara jolts awake, panting, her trembling hand still holding in her voice.

* * *

There's a thumping from someplace far away and Clara groans. She'd been having that dream again. She remembers waking up next to Dean after having this dream and shrinking away from him, making herself as small and quiet as possible, balancing on the edge of the bed so he couldn't reach out and stroke her back in his sleep.

Her eyes close tighter, but her phone pings, and she gropes around on the bed before realizing it's plugged into the charger on her nightstand.

Chris's message, *You home?* glows at the top of her notifications. He knows she is. He has a key, too, but she knows he won't barge in.

She unlocks her phone and types, *No.*

Chris replies before she can put the phone back down. *Yes, you are.* And then, *Hungry?*

Is she? She doesn't know. Her tongue is still swollen, but the pain in her head has dulled. She wonders if she's been sleep-drinking from the sink, her body unconsciously driven to survive despite her ego's attempts to make it suffer. She crawls to the foot of the bed and tests her balance before lurching into the bathroom. She tosses her phone onto the counter, turns the cold tap on full blast, and sticks her whole face under the faucet, lapping at the stream like the cat sometimes does.

Her phone pings again. *I'm coming in okay?*

K.

Clara hears the creak of the front door as she's changing her stale, damp clothes for something only slightly less dingy, ignoring the overflowing hamper in the closet.

By the time she makes it downstairs, Chris has fed the cat and set up Styrofoam containers of Chinese takeout on the coffee table. He opens a package of chopsticks and sets them on top of one of the containers.

When he notices Clara, he gestures toward the food and says, "Hey." The cat is watching from the tv stand, licking his lips.

"Thanks," Clara says as she sits cross-legged on the floor in front of the food. It smells spicy and humid. Like bile. She's never really hungry anymore and hates to admit it when she is. Mostly she's nauseous. The way you are when you're sick to your stomach but nothing's moving in either direction, and you're afraid to put anything in your mouth. She doesn't know if she can eat, but she knows she should try. People expect that.

She picks up the chopsticks but can't figure out how to hold them. It's not like she's never used them before; they used to get sushi every Saturday. Well, every Saturday they could afford to, and Dean always insisted she not use a fork or her fingers. But now her stupid fingers don't know what to do with the two slender sticks in her hand, and Clara feels her throat clench, swallowing a sob. Or a gag.

Chris, whom Clara once described to her sister as aloof and utterly oblivious, places one calloused hand on Clara's shoulder, lays a fork on top of her napkin, and removes the chopsticks from her open palms. He doesn't say a word, and his touch is like a knitted shawl on a chilly night. A whispered tenderness that reminds her that she's still alive.

* * *

It wasn't until after Dean died that Clara realized how few people she'd stayed in touch with over the years. Her closest friends really only work acquaintances good for a cocktail once in a while after work and the usual bitch session about what what's-her-face did that pissed off some other so-and-so. The people she knew from high school and college had all gone their separate ways, and she'd always had convenient excuses for avoiding reunions. Clara can't help but wonder if she's even remembered when the only connections she's maintained are brief birthday wishes on Facebook on the rare occasions she bothers to check her feed.

When everything was happening so fast after the crash and the hospital, it was Clara's sister who'd materialized by her side, dropping everything to catch the next flight out of Dallas. Mal helped make funeral arrangements, make calls, make sure Clara slept, ate, showered. But not long after, Mal had to return to her own life. To her husband. Her children. And Clara was alone again. Mostly.

Her parents came up for the funeral to stare at her with watery eyes and hug her over and over as words continued to fail them. At the reception, held in a respectable banquet room and decorated by Mal in crushed velvet blues and greys, Clara watched her mother taking nervous gulps of chardonnay as people—only some Clara recognized as old friends or relatives —gave their condolences. It was all strange and unnatural, and Clara still hoped she'd wake up and realize it was all a night-mare. She had trouble hearing the "I'm so sorrys" and "If you ever need anythings." She said the usual things she thought a widow was expected to say.

Dean was such a good man. He didn't deserve this. She didn't know if she could go on without him.

And she hid inside herself, waiting for the moment someone would call her a liar.

Toward the end of the reception, Clara's mother stood from a faux marble bench embossed with tiny, trumpet-playing cher-ubs and wobbled toward her. She sloshed her stemless wine glass as she bent to whisper-shout in Clara's ear, "It's too bad he didn't freeze any sperm." Then, blinking, "Did he freeze any sperm?"

Clara could only stare at her mother, a scream trapped inside her head and vomit in her throat, until her father gripped her mother's elbow and directed her toward the half-empty food trays.

* * *

Letting out a jagged breath, Clara picks up the fork and opens the food container, which is overflowing with spicy lo mien and white rice. She wants to thank Chris for being here, for continuing to be here, but she is afraid her body will betray her. Instead, she pokes at her rice and attempts a smile in his direction.

Chris nods and turns on the tv. He spends some time choosing a channel with sounds suitable to fill the space, to blanketing their shared sorrow. Nothing too serious or too funny. But as he scrolls through On Demand, he begins to laugh. It starts as a sort of chuff. It's barely a sound at all. He looks at Clara, and when their eyes meet, he loses himself. He holds his chest and doubles over with laughter.

"What the fuck is wrong with you?" Clara asks.

Chris can only laugh harder, falling onto his side, into Clara's shoulder, tears streaming down his cheeks. His face is contorted with disgust, and the wails of confusion she's been denying herself pour out of his mouth. She cradles the head of her dead husband's best friend in a kind of numb terror.

When he starts apologizing in a breathless, little boy's hiccupping whimper, she shushes him like he's a sick toddler, rocking him, telling him it's okay. She tilts her face to the ceiling and blinks so her own tears won't fall into Chris's messy brown curls.

They sit like this for a long time. Long enough for the food to go cold and the room to go gray. When Chris sits up, the air feels lighter, wrung out.

He says, "I didn't mean for that to happen. I just can't." He doesn't say what he can't, but that's okay because neither can Clara. She isn't ready. Doesn't know if she'll ever be ready for that.

"Remember that time," Chris says, "when I got Dean to hold Maddie?"

The first time Chris brought his daughter over, she was only a few months old. He hadn't wanted to put her down and said things like, "You never realize until she's right there, man. She's beautiful. I'd do anything for her." Dean had shaken his head and put his palms out, but Chris had plopped Maddie into Dean's arms as if to force the sublimity of fatherhood. Dean had gripped the baby at her armpits and held her at arms' length, grimacing in psychological pain, until she spit upon his thumb and Chris took her back.

"Yeah," Clara says. "I remember."

She goes into the kitchen and pulls a pack of Camel Lights and a lighter from where she'd hidden them in the junk drawer. She lights up right there and slides up onto the counter. She watches Chris pick up the remote and continue his channel surfing. The cat creeps onto the couch and headbutts Chris's shoulder. Clara can hear the damn thing purring as she ashes into the sink.

And Then They Were There

DAVE SIMS

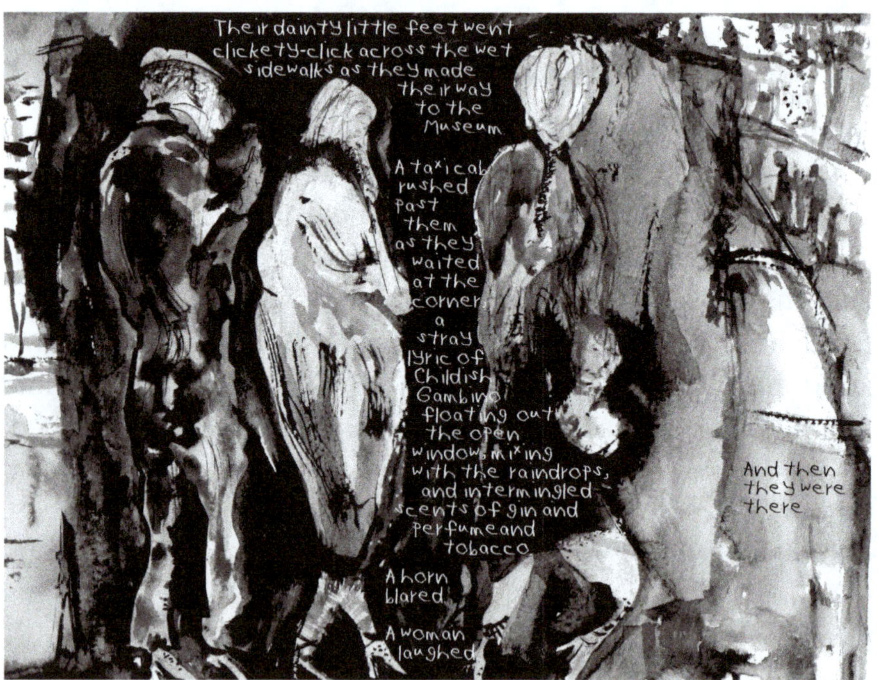

And Then They Were There, from the Sudden Awakenings Collection, 2021-
Mixed Media; Word-Image Hybrid
Dave Sims

Two Poems: cactus and vines

J.E. O'LEARY

cactus

pain is a desert - arid, long, so long. wide.
unending. we are judged here by our minimums:
rainfall, population, grief.

tearing open plants for their water, there is something sweet
    inside.

in college i kept cacti in little clay pots.
they wilted in the a/c so i left them on the front steps.
like sentries.

they flourished in the high desert - talked with the wind,
fended off small critters, bided their time.
i wondered if they could
tell the difference between the captivity of being
tied to the soil, in the wild,
and the humiliating captivity of a pot.

i had to move out suddenly, and could not take
nor settle, everything.

when the day came i loaded my last bag - my laundry -
into the back seat and saw them - one tall, lean,
one stout - round. i'd called them abbot and costello.

low maintenance as they were, i imagined
they could live satisfactorily for weeks,
before they over realized i was gone

they seemed to sway in the oppressive sun, waving goodbye,
but of course it was an illusion. we see what we want to see,
always have

many years later by chance i found myself back in NM
and took a severe detour in order to check out the old place.
there were plants on the porch, but no cacti.
the shutters had been painted burnt orange.
the house looked lived in but empty,
gentle air circulating.

i leaned on my car, an iced coffee shaking
against my restless quad.

vines

i'm trapped in the vines of things
that grow on vines

and snack on the fruits of the vines
that trap
choke
wrap
and otherwise constrict

well what comes next but thorns
and assimilation?

they get you but unfortunately
they take you too-
raise you through
several planets' airs and
make you life,
but you make them stairs.

i'm trapped in the vines of vines
that grow on buildings,
splayed against cool brick
like an artistic curiosity
that is not breaking through the noise

coeds walk under me in the fall
with their sweaters and their hormones
and their whole pink lives ahead of them

i'm trapped in the vines of things that
grow on vines, predicting
the subtle pain in your side
the fingertips pat your skin for scratches
and prepare you
to be studied under the light
of the insurgent moon

The Garden at Evenstrock

PHYLLIS GREEN

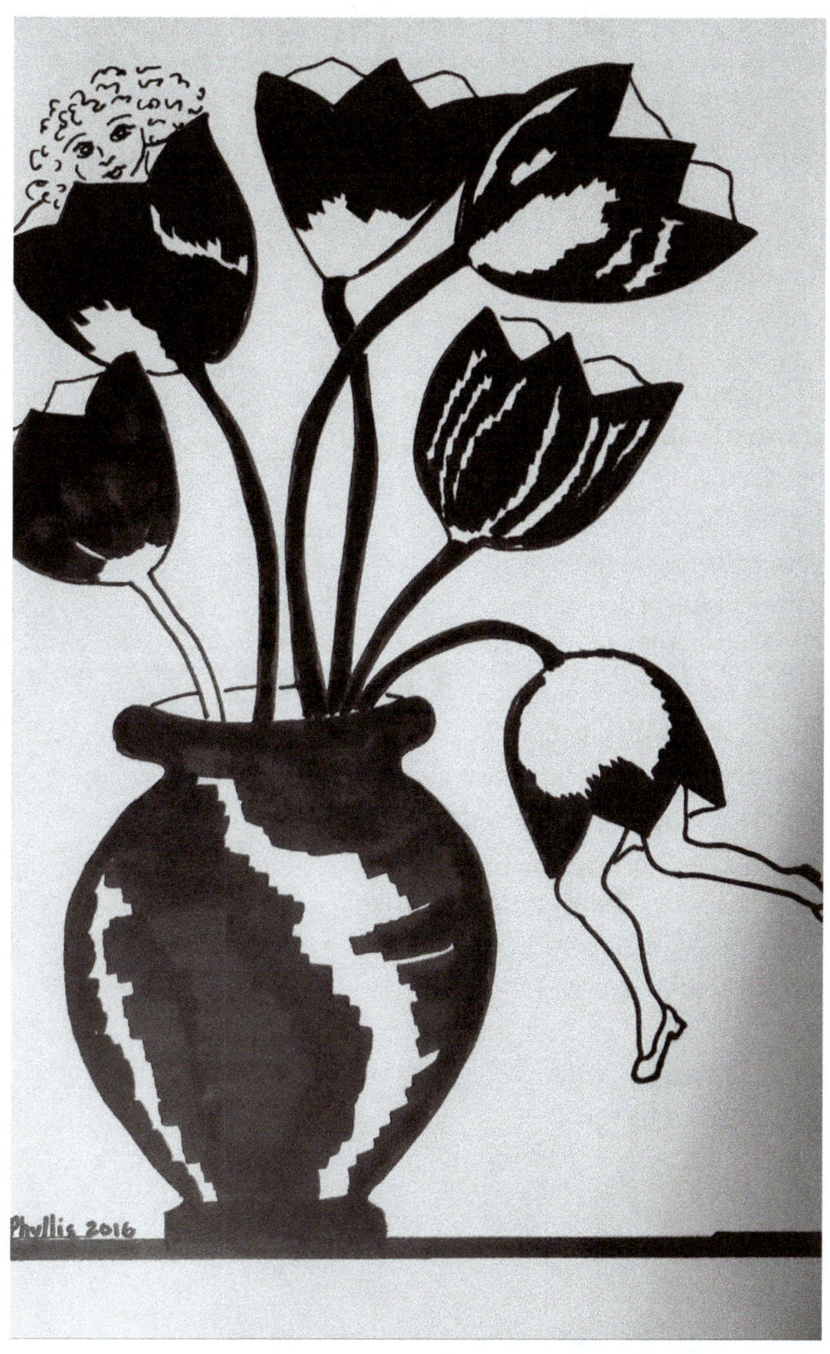

From The Garden at Evenstrock Collection, 2016 - Black
marker drawn on illustration art boards (9 x 12)
Phyllis Green

Purple Heart

LORETTA TOBIN

The Purple Heart he wears
pinned on his uniform
means wounded in action.

No other visible clue
alerts us to the damage
hidden under his clothes,

from the bullet hole
that healed with an uneven red welt.
At night when he sleeps,

perspiration dampens his pillow
and he twitches and twists,
pulling all the covers

away from his wife.
She wants to know—
will his scars ever fade?

Little Things

NICHOLAS A. BRUSH

Amongst all the noise and all the chatter,
It doesn't take long for us to forget
it's the little things that really matter.

The din's. Non. Stop. The clamor and clatter
compose grotesque, dissonant silhouettes.
Amongst all the noise and all the chatter,

Thank you for your service is a dagger
in the soul. Don't treat me like an outlet
for the little things that really matter,

like housing. Employment. Don't you flatter
me with song while so many of our vets,
Amongst all the noise and all the chatter,

wait, and wait, and wait, and write their chapters
on VA forms. 214? You can bet
that's a little thing that really matters.

Fill out one form and the stack gets fatter
every time. I need a fucking cigarette.
Amongst all the noise and all the chatter,
it's the little things that really matter.

Harmonious Healer

SUZANNE COTTRELL

Turquoise connects sky blues to aquamarine seas,
life giving elements of air and water.
As my self-confidence ebbs and flows,
I seek seclusion on a tropical island
surrounded by soothing, tepid, blue-green waters.
Rainbow and tetra fish shimmer
peacefully beneath the surface.
Rhythmic waves lap, spiritual lullabies,
attempt to calm my inner turmoil.

My thoughts churn like ocean surf
until wisdom glows, resembles
dazzling, bioluminescence swirls
I taste, smell salty spray,
transport myself to pristine Alaskan waters.
Stunning, Turquoise tinted, glacial ice
awakens my emotions as
ice calves into northern waters.
My worries break off, drift away,
melt in warmer seas.

Turquoise, a master healer,
that adorns my physical being
while it purifies my mind,
realigns my energy,
restores my inner harmony.

Fusion

TIMOTHY F. PHILLIPS

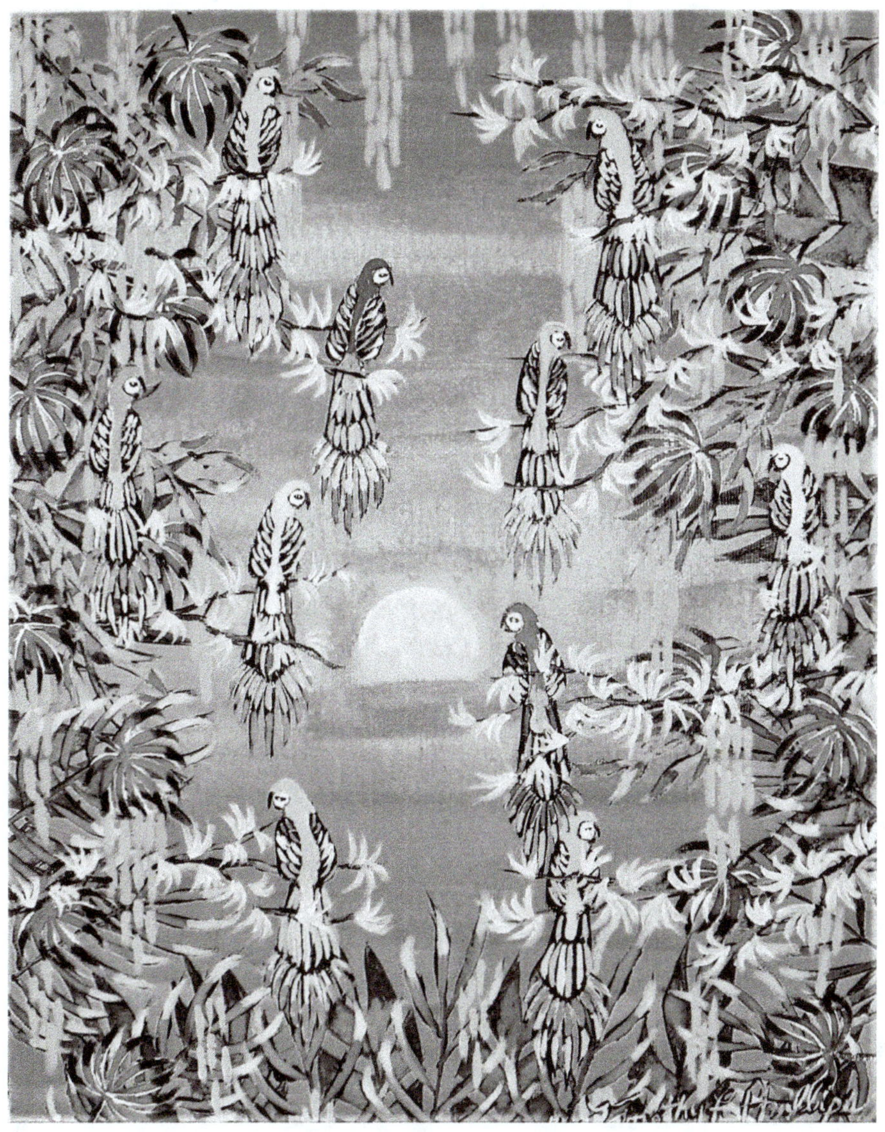

Fusion, 2018 - Acrylic on Canvas (11x14)
Timothy Phillips

Biographies

Erika Maria is an artist based in Brooklyn, New York. From a young age, Erika expressed herself creatively through drawing. She received her Bachelor's in Graphic Design at the Art Institute of Fort Lauderdale and continued to work in the field for 13 years. Ultimately, Erika found it not to be her true passion. She decided to take her first oil painting class in September of 2018 at the School of Visual Arts. Oil painting gave her the confidence to take her life-long passion more seriously. She has since been working on mastering her technique to further improve and evolve her style in portraiture, figurative, and still life painting.

Katherine Gaffney completed her MFA at the University of Illinois at Urbana-Champaign and is currently working on her PhD at the University of Southern Mississippi. Her work has previously appeared or is forthcoming in *jubilat*, *Rabbit Catastrophe*, *Harpur Palate*, the *Mississippi Review*, *Meridian*, the *Tampa Review*, and elsewhere.

David Zarko was founding artistic director of The Metropolitan Playhouse of New York, 1991 through 2000 then producing artistic director of Scranton, Pennsylvania's Electric Theatre Company until 2011. He has over 90 professional directing credits plus more than 50 in academic theatre, and has taught (and directed) at C.W. Post L.I.U., American Academy of Dramatic Arts, Marywood University, and others. He's also a produced playwright, sometimes actor, and a member of The Dramatists Guild and Society of Stage Directors and Choreographers.

Olga Nenazhivna is a Russian/American artist, art curator, and educator. She received her initial artistic training under her father, a professional sculptor, and her mother, an art enthusiast followed by the formal education receiving a Bachelor of Fine Arts. A child prodigy, she received her first best art award at the age of five and had her first solo show at the age of ten at the Gallery of the Union of Artists of Russia. Since then, she has exhibited her work not only in Russia but also in Japan, Canada, the UK, and the USA. Processing powerful pictorial imagination, excellent old-school technique, and superb taste, Olga Nenazhivina creates graphic work, which aesthetics are a fine merger of the East and West.

Kaitlin Kan is a student at Yale University studying literature and psychology. Hailing from the suburbs of Philadelphia with Chinese ancestry, her writing draws from rich cultural ties, as well as from her extensive experiences with mental illness. She is currently working on a poetry chapbook exploring the intersections between storytelling and corporeality.

Jack Bordnick's interest are to create artistic, meaningful works of art that can be enjoyed by all peoples and cultures. Being a designer and sculptor, has allowed him to share my professional experiences, in a beneficial way for both business and community projects of this nature. He has been a successful designer and have over twenty years experience in design, fabrication and installation of numerous and diverse projects of this nature. An Industrial designer/Sculptor graduate of Pratt Institute in New York, where he has had his own professional design business and been a design director for numerous companies and local government projects. They included a major children's museum, for the city of New York and Board of Education. Being a designer and sculptor living here in New Mexico, has allowed him to have a deep understanding of our culture and environment, that has influenced his artistic interpretation and creative solutions to design projects. This is what he enjoys sharing with all peoples.

Angel Baker is a poet in Southern California with publications in *MoonTide Press*, *The Northridge Review*, *Jelly Bucket*, and *Poets.org*. Baker has published articles, reviews, interviews, and essays in various digital and print magazines in Los Angeles, San Francisco, and New York. Angel is the 2019 recipient of the Academy of American Poets Prize for the poem, "Vista, California," selected by poet and judge Anna Journey.

Robert McGuill's work has appeared in *Narrative*, the *Southwest Review*, the *Saturday Evening Post*, *Louisiana Literature*, *American Fiction* and other publications. His stories have been nominated for the Pushcart Prize five times, and short-listed for awards by, among others, *Glimmer Train*, the *New Guard*, *Sequestrum Art & Literature*.

Beatle Darcy is a Junior and an English major at Colorado College. She is originally from Northern New Jersey but moved to a small farm in New Hampshire before high school. You can most likely find Beatle in the woods, out in the garden, or reading a book with a cup of tea by the fire.

Peter Serchuk's poems of have appeared in *New Letters*, *Poetry*, *Denver Quarterly*, *Boulevard*, *Booth*, *Texas Review* and other places. A new collection of poems and photographs, "The Purpose of Things," (in collaboration with photographer Pieter de Koninck) will appear in 2020 from Regal House Publishing.

Zahr Said is an Arab-American law professor who writes about copyright law, conceptual art, craft beer, Arab and African literature and the politics of voice in *Hamilton: an American Musical.* Somehow it all hangs together; she is currently working on a memoir about how it does. Follow her on Twitter: @zahr_said.

Anthony J. Mohr's work has appeared in, among other places, *DIAGRAM*, *Green Hills Literary Lantern*, *Hippocampus Magazine*, *North Dakota Quarterly*, *Maryland Literary Review*, *Saint Ann's Review*, *Superstition Review*, *ZYZZYVA*, and several anthologies. He has been nominated five times for the Pushcart Prize, received honorable mention in Sequestrum's 2016 Editor's Reprint Award, and was a finalist in Living Springs Publishers' 2019 Stories Through the Ages contest. He has been a guest writer on several blogs, including Brevity, and is an assistant editor of *Evening Street Review*. Currently, he is a fellow in the Advanced Leadership Initiative at Harvard.

Laura Ohlmann is an MFA graduate from the University of Central Florida. Her work is forthcoming in *The Rumpus* and has appeared in and *The Maine Review*, *Honey&Lime*, *South Florida Poetry Journal*, *In Parentheses*, *The Elevation Review* and was an honorable mention in 2016 Wild Ekphrastic Poetry Contest. She enjoys sleeping in her converted Honda Element and biking up mountains with her partner and dog.

Mary Buchinger is the author of four collections of poetry, including *e i n f ü h l u n g/in feeling*, *Aerialist*, and *Navigating the Reach* (forthcoming). She is president of the New England Poetry Club and professor of English and communication studies at MCPHS University in Boston. (www.marybuchinger.com).

Bryan Starchman is an author living in San Francisco, California. His plays have been produced over 3000 times in all 50 states and 10 countries. In the past year his short fiction has been featured in *The Saturday Evening Post* and in the literary journals *After Dinner Conversation*, *In Parentheses*, *Scribble*, *Apracity*, *Avalon Literary Review*, *The Good Life Review*, and

Litro. Learn more about Bryan at www.bryanstarchman.com, or follow him on Instagram @bryan.starchman.

Robert Ball graduated with a bachelor's degree in writing from Northern Michigan University. While attending, he worked as an editing intern for *Passages North* literary magazine and currently works professionally as a technical editor. His fiction has appeared in *Third Point Press*, *Prometheus Dreaming*, and *Button Eye Review* and has been nominated for the PEN/ Robert J. Dau Short Story Prize and the Pushcart Prize.

Tara Iacobucci is a mother of three living in the Boston area, and she teaches high school English. She self-published a young adult fiction novel titled *The Trouble with Pretty*, and her poetry has recently appeared in *Mothers Always Write* and *The Bangalore Review*.

Anna Mantzaris lives in San Francisco. Her work has appeared in publications including *Ambit*, *The Cortland Review* and *Mc-Sweeney's Internet Tendency*. Her short story collection 'The Girl Who Can Take the Most Electricity' was a finalist for the 2020 Eyelands Book Award. She has been awarded residencies for her writing by Hedgebrook and The Kimmel Harding Nelson Center for the Arts.

Tobi Alfier is a multiple Pushcart nominee and multiple Best of the Net nominee. "Symmetry: earth and sky" was published by *Main Street Rag*. Her chapbook "Grit & Grace" is forthcoming from Orchard Street Press. She is co-editor of *San Pedro River Review* (www.bluehorsepress.com).

Anne Rudig was born in San Francisco and adopted by a socially prominent California family. She grew up in the Bay Area and received a B.A. from the University of California at Berkeley before moving to New York to pursue a career in dance. After several years of performing as a modern dancer, she obtained a B.F.A. in communication design from Parsons School of Design. Anne worked on Madison Avenue on the "I Love New York" campaign, spent over twenty years in advertising as a writer, art director and creative director, and became Director of Communication for the Episcopal Church worldwide. In 2018, Anne received an M.F.A. in Writing from Columbia University, where the first draft of this memoir was completed. Anne wrote about her experiences at Columbia in a piece for The *New York Times*, "Back to School, at 64." She lives in northwestern Connecticut with her husband.

McKenzie Zalopany is an instructor and MFA student at the University of South Florida. Her work has been published at *The Boiler, Superstition Review, Tulane Review* and elsewhere. Her work centers around gender, motherhood, and disability advocacy.

Courtney Lee Hall has been published with *TulipTree Publishing* and *Tiny Seed Literary Journal*. She lives in Arizona with her face always towards the sun.

Liliana Rehorn's work has previously appeared or is forthcoming in such publications as *Bayou Magazine* and *Opiate Magazine*. Rehorn was the winner of the 2019 JuxtaProse Poetry Prize. Liliana currently lives in Southern California and is working on a collection of poetry.

Roger Camp is the author of three photography books including the award-winning *Butterflies in Flight,* Thames & Hudson, 2002 and *Heat*, Charta, Milano, 2008. His work has appeared on the covers of numerous journals including *The New England Review, Southwest Review*, and *Vassar Review*. His documentary photography has been awarded Europe's prestigious Leica Medal of Excellence. His photographs are represented by the

Robin Rice Gallery, NYC. More of his images may be seen on Luminous-Lint.com.

Stephanie Lamb began writing as a teen, but in her mid 20's went through a medication-induced writers block and rediscovered her voice about a decade later. Now she writes to empower others and give a voice to the voiceless. You can find Stephanie on Instagram and Facebook @stephanielambpoetry. Other singular pieces have been published by *Weasel Press*, *io Literary Journal*, *Poets Unlimited Mag* and *Divine Feminist Anthology*.

Richard Fouts is a San Diego playwright and a recent transplant from New York City. His first full-length work, *The Birthday Lottery*, a new play about the Vietnam draft, premiered at Z-Space, San Francisco's premiere theatre for new works, to sold-out audiences in 2018. Since then, Fouts has written *My Afternoon With Lenny* (a light comedy about Leonard Bernstein), *Dead Serious* (a dark comedy about two female assassins) and is developing his short play, "Summer Me, Winter Me" (a drama about a composer and his opera-singer wife) into a full-length play.

Gloria Keely is a graduate of San Francisco State University with a BA and MA in Creative Writing. Gloria has recently begun taking photos for publication in 2020.

Holly Day (hollylday.blogspot.com) has been a writing instructor at the Loft Literary Center in Minneapolis since 2000. Her poetry has recently appeared in *Hubbub*, *Grain*, and *Third Wednesday*, and her newest books are *The Tooth is the Largest Organ in the Human Body* (Anaphora Literary Press), *Book of Beasts* (Weasel Press), *Bound in Ice* (Shanti Arts), and *Music Composition for Dummies* (Wiley).

R. E. Sawyer lives in the Pacific Northwest with her partner and three cats. She teaches middle school language arts in her spare time.

Dave Sims is a retired educator who now makes art and music in the old mountains of central Pennsylvania. His traditional and digital paintings and comix appear in dozens of tangible and virtual publications, galleries, and exhibits, with new work forthcoming in *Sunspot Literature*, *Raw Art Review* and *The Abstract Elephant*. Experience more at www.tincansims.com

J.E. O'Leary is a songwriter, stage performer, poet and visual artist from NYC. For over 20 years, largely performing under the stagename Joe Yoga, he has been bringing his music and art to NYC's stages, festivals, subway platforms, and gallery walls. He has performed at the Nuyorican Poets Café, the New York Poetry Festival, KGB Bar, and at numerous other poetry shows. Musically, his unique songwriting style and passionate performances have made him and favorite of and a fixture at venues across the city.

Phyllis Green's art has appeared in *ArLiJo 123*, the *Revolution, Earth & Altar*, and soon in *Thereafter* and *Superpresent*.

Loretta Tobin was born and raised in rural North Dakota. Her formal education started in a one- room school without running water. She graduated from Minnesota State University—Moorhead with a B.S.Ed. She lives in Everett, Washington with her husband. She retired from the City of Everett and the U.S. Navy Reserve. Her Navy assignments included a tour in Al Asad, Iraq. Her early life experiences that had more in common with the early 1900s than today and going off to war profoundly influenced her and provided her with writing material.

Nicholas A. Brush is a PhD student in Renaissance Literature at the University of North Texas. Even though his current scholarship lies in Early Modern drama, poetry is his first love. Nicholas's poetry has been published in multiple journals, as well as being included in an anthology for Lawton, Oklahoma writers. His first poetry collection is still in progress, but he hopes to finish it some time within the next decade.

Suzanne Cottrell, an Ohio buckeye by birth, lives with her husband and three rescued dogs in rural Piedmont North Carolina. An outdoor enthusiast and retired teacher, she enjoys reading, writing, hiking, knitting, Pilates, and yoga. Her poems have appeared in numerous journals and anthologies including *Best Emerging Poets Series*, *Avocet*, *Poetry Quarterly*, *The Pangolin Review*, and *Burningword Literary Journal*. She was the recipient of the 2017 Rebecca Lard Poetry Award, Prolific Press. Author's website: https://suzanneswords.com.

Timothy F. Phillips art is considered to be a naive artist with a splash of realism And little cats become symbols that transmit that 'another reality is hidden behind appearances,' and enchanted paths to the beach come to suggest evocative images of a better world for all to enjoy and live in contentment. Occasionally he frames his vision of the artwork with bright foliage through which the skies glimmer and the moons glow in an evening hue. Timothy believes that with the publication of his words and his works he is bringing to light the essence of the work of a true master who achieves with his art a transformation not of the world, but of the way we see it. for this and many other reasons, when one speaks of Timothy F Phillips, we do so of an artist truly committed to the body of work - composed with a precise hand and great use of colors and hues, shading, and shapes, and forms, - which brings us a vision of a more human world we are in.

SUBMISSION INFORMATION

New Plains Review accepts original work in poetry, prose, and visual art. Submission information and editorial guidelines are accessible through our website newplainsreview.com and via Submittable at https://newplainsreview.submittable.com

ORDERING INFORMATION

Pricing for current and back issues is available through Amazon.